Corporate Governance

Sustainability Policies and Practices for Corporate Governance in Brazil

OECD

BETTER POLICIES FOR BETTER LIVES

This work is published under the responsibility of the Secretary-General of the OECD. The opinions expressed and arguments employed herein do not necessarily reflect the official views of the Member countries of the OECD.

This document, as well as any data and map included herein, are without prejudice to the status of or sovereignty over any territory, to the delimitation of international frontiers and boundaries and to the name of any territory, city or area.

The statistical data for Israel are supplied by and under the responsibility of the relevant Israeli authorities. The use of such data by the OECD is without prejudice to the status of the Golan Heights, East Jerusalem and Israeli settlements in the West Bank under the terms of international law.

Note by Turkey
The information in this document with reference to "Cyprus" relates to the southern part of the Island. There is no single authority representing both Turkish and Greek Cypriot people on the Island. Turkey recognises the Turkish Republic of Northern Cyprus (TRNC). Until a lasting and equitable solution is found within the context of the United Nations, Turkey shall preserve its position concerning the "Cyprus issue".

Note by all the European Union Member States of the OECD and the European Union
The Republic of Cyprus is recognised by all members of the United Nations with the exception of Turkey. The information in this document relates to the area under the effective control of the Government of the Republic of Cyprus.

Please cite this publication as:
OECD (2022), *Sustainability Policies and Practices for Corporate Governance in Brazil*, Corporate Governance, OECD Publishing, Paris, https://doi.org/10.1787/a9889ba3-en.

ISBN 978-92-64-85211-2 (print)
ISBN 978-92-64-82219-1 (pdf)
ISBN 978-92-64-55885-4 (HTML)
ISBN 978-92-64-42669-6 (epub)

Corporate Governance
ISSN 2077-6527 (print)
ISSN 2077-6535 (online)

Foreword

Brazil is looking to improve its sustainability policies for corporate governance with a view to aligning its legal and regulatory framework with the recommendations in the G20/OECD Principles of Corporate Governance (G20/OECD Principles).

This report contributes to this goal by presenting an overview of the main trends and issues related to sustainability policies and practices for corporate governance, both in Brazil and globally. It supports efforts to develop the country's legal and regulatory framework for sustainability disclosure, the responsibilities of company boards and shareholder rights. The analysis in the report is based on responses to two OECD surveys with 63 Brazilian companies comprising around half of the country's market capitalisation and 363 asset managers investing more than USD 1 trillion in the country.

This report is part of a joint project between the OECD and Brazil's Securities and Exchange Commission (Comissão de Valores Mobiliários - CVM) and funded by the UK Prosperity Fund. The project is divided into two phases. This report concludes the first phase of data collection and analysis. In the second phase, the OECD will organise an experts' workshop in Brazil and further develop the findings in this report to include policy recommendations.

This report was prepared by Caio Figueiredo Cibella de Oliveira and Tugba Mulazimoglu, under the supervision of Serdar Çelik, all from the Corporate Governance and Corporate Finance Division of the OECD Directorate for Financial and Enterprise Affairs. It benefits from and includes some extracts from a new OECD report on *Climate Change and Corporate Governance*. The authors are grateful to Alejandra Medina for valuable comments and to Greta Gabbarini for communications support.

Table of contents

FIGURES

TABLES

Follow OECD Publications on:

http://twitter.com/OECD_Pubs

http://www.facebook.com/OECDPublications

http://www.linkedin.com/groups/OECD-Publications-4645871

http://www.youtube.com/oecdilibrary

OECD Alerts http://www.oecd.org/oecddirect/

Acronyms and abbreviations

ABRASCA	Brazilian Association of Public Companies	IPCC	Intergovernmental Panel on Climate Change
AICPA	American Institute of Certified Public Accountants	IPO	initial public offerings
ANBIMA	Brazilian Financial and Capital Markets Association	IR	Integrated Reporting
AUM	assets under management	ISSB	International Sustainability Standards Board
BCB	Central Bank of Brazil	ITMO	Internationally Traded Mitigation Outcome
BMF SA	Brazilian Mercantile & Futures Exchange	LSE	London School of Economics
CDP	Carbon Disclosure Project	MNE	Multinational Enterprise
CDSB	Climate Disclosure Standards Boards	NDC	nationally determined contribution
CVM	Securities and Exchange Commission of Brazil	NFRD	Non-Financial Reporting Directive
EM	emerging markets	OECD	Organisation for Economic Co-operation and Development
ESG	environmental, social and governance	OTC	over the counter
ETS	emission trading system	PBC	public benefit corporation
EU	European Union	R&D	research and development
FASB	Financial Accounting Standards Board	ROA	return on assets
FSB	Financial Stability Board	ROE	return on equity
GDP	gross domestic product	REIT	Real Estate Investment Trust
GHG	Greenhouse Gases	SASB	Sustainability Accounting Standards Board
GRI	Global Reporting Initiative	SEC	Securities and Exchange Commission of the United States
GSI	Global Sustainability Initiative	SLB	sustainability-linked bonds
GSSB	Global Sustainability Standards Board	SME	small and medium-sized enterprise
IAASB	International Auditing and Assurance Standards Board	SPO	secondary public offerings
IASB	International Accounting Standards Board	TCFD	Task Force on Climate-related Financial Disclosures
IBOVESPA	The Bovespa Index	TRWG	Technical Readiness Working Group
IFAC	International Federation of Accountants	TSVCM	Taskforce on Scaling Voluntary Carbon Markets
IFRS	International Accounting Standards Board	UN	United Nations
ILO	International Labour Organization	VRF	Value Reporting Foundation
IOSCO	International Organization of Securities Commissions	WEF	World Economic Forum

Executive summary

This report presents an overview of the main trends and issues related to sustainability policies and practices for corporate governance, both in Brazil and globally. It serves to support the development of Brazil's regulatory framework for sustainability disclosure, the responsibilities of company boards and shareholder rights. The report presents the results of two OECD surveys conducted with 63 Brazilian companies comprising around half of the country's stock market capitalisation and 363 asset managers investing more than USD 1 trillion in the country.

Brazil's capital market landscape. Brazil's public equity market had 190 new listings and 542 delistings from 2000 to 2020. Net listings were only positive in 2007 and in 2020. Total market capitalisation represented 68% of GDP at the end of 2020, which was lower than in the United States (194%), the United Kingdom (149%) and India (98%), but higher than in Mexico (37%).

Private corporations were the most important category of equity owners in Brazil with 29% of market at the end of 2020. They were followed by institutional investors (27%), the public sector (10%) and strategic individuals (8%). Foreign investors managed 65% of the equity owned by institutional investors. The average combined holdings of the top three shareholders in Brazil represents 57% of a company's equity, which is similar to the ownership concentration in France, India and Mexico, but considerably higher than in the United Kingdom (36%) and in the United States (33%).

Brazilian companies raised a total of USD 864 billion in bonds from 2000 to 2021, with 60% of this amount issued by non-financial companies. There were 35 issuers of green bonds in Brazil in the same period, among which 23 are either listed or subsidiaries of listed companies. Green bond issuance, however, totalled only USD 8.2 billion, close to the amounts issued in India and Mexico but considerably smaller than in other markets (e.g. USD 64.4 billion in the United Kingdom).

Corporate disclosure. A majority of asset managers investing in Brazil review the sustainability disclosure of the companies in their portfolios. For large asset managers, 59% report that they review the sustainability disclosure from all investee companies and 29% that they do so only for certain industries. Every year, Brazilian public companies must either disclose a sustainability report or explain why they do not disclose one. The companies that disclose a sustainability report may choose to use any existing sustainability accounting standard.

To date, a number of reporting standards have been developed for companies to disclose sustainability information but these standards vary with respect to their target audiences, the issues they cover and the threshold they recommend for information to be disclosed. In Brazil, the GRI Standards are the most-often used sustainability standards, but other frameworks, such as the SASB Standards, are also used by many public companies. This multitude of existing standards, however, raises questions related to the comparability of sustainability information disclosed by companies. This is probably the reason why a majority of asset managers investing in Brazil and public companies in the country would support the adoption of an international sustainability reporting standard for listed companies (71% support from large asset managers and 76% from large companies).

The use of multiple sustainability reporting standards is not the only barrier to greater consistency and comparability of corporate sustainability disclosure. When the sustainability information disclosed is not assured by a third party based on robust methodologies, confidence in the information can be undermined. In Brazil, 76% of large listed companies that disclose sustainability information provide some level of assurance by a third party, but this is much lower for smaller companies (25%).

The responsibility of boards. While business reality is complex, corporate law generally presents a simplified definition of directors' duties, including the duties of care and loyalty, in order to make them functional. Jurisdictions vary in relation to who is effectively the recipient of directors' duty of loyalty between the following two extremes:

- At one end of the spectrum, company law may fully adhere to the "shareholder primacy" view, obliging directors to consider only shareholders' financial interests while complying with the applicable law and ethical standards.
- At the other end of the spectrum, directors are required to balance shareholders' financial interests with the best interests of stakeholders, and, in addition, to fulfil a number of public interest goals.

Brazil's company law adopts a model that may be situated between those two extremes. Independent of these considerations, a large majority of boards of directors in Brazil considered sustainability matters in 2021 (human capital and data security were the top priorities). Companies for who climate change is a financially material risk represented 70% of market capitalisation in Brazil in 2021 – 5 percentage points above the global average. Executive compensation plans were linked to sustainability performance metrics in 79% of large public companies and in 21% of the smaller companies in 2021.

Shareholders rights and engagement. Shareholders commonly use three main fora to compel companies to incorporate sustainability-related considerations into their business decision-making processes: direct dialogue with directors and key executives, shareholder meetings and courts. A large majority of asset managers investing in Brazil consider sustainability risks and opportunities when voting in a shareholder meeting or engaging with directors (e.g. 82% of large asset managers when in dialogue with directors and executives). Interestingly, a majority of asset managers declared to be willing to accept a lower rate of return in a company in exchange for societal or environmental benefits. From 2019 to 2021, at least 33 sustainability-related shareholder resolutions were voted in a shareholder meeting in Brazil. Human capital, climate change, biodiversity and data security were the most frequent sustainability matters considered in these resolutions.

While litigation involving shareholder rights is uncommon in Brazil, the rupture of a Vale tailings dam in the city of Brumadinho in 2019 has given rise to six arbitrations before the arbitration chamber of the local stock exchange by (i) 385 minority shareholders, (ii) a class association of minority shareholders and (iii) foreign investment funds. Brazil's Securities and Exchange Commission has also initiated an administrative proceeding to assess Vale's key executives' fulfilment of their duty of care in events related to the rupture of the dam in Brumadinho, and the indictment has yet to be evaluated by the Commissioners.

1 Introduction

This chapter first summarises the outline of the report and then provides an overview of the profile of the respondents to the two OECD surveys on practices and approaches on corporate sustainability in Brazil: (1) survey of public companies registered with the Brazilian securities regulator and (2) survey of asset managers investing in Brazil.

This publication is the output of a joint project involving the OECD and Brazil's Securities and Exchange Commission (*Comissão de Valores Mobiliários* – CVM) to support the development of capital market regulation related to sustainability risks faced by listed companies. It provides an overview of the main trends and issues related to sustainability and corporate governance in the country and at the global level. Its goal is to support the development of the country's framework for sustainability disclosure, the responsibilities of company boards and shareholder rights in alignment with the G20/OECD Principles of Corporate Governance (G20/OECD Principles).

The jurisdictions whose frameworks and markets are covered in this report include Brazil, France, India, Mexico, the United States and the United Kingdom. The selection of those countries was based on multiple criteria, including comparable sizes of their economies, diversity of regions and the effectiveness of the existing frameworks in some of those jurisdictions.

This chapter presents the profile of the respondents to the two OECD surveys on practices and approaches on corporate sustainability in Brazil: (1) survey of public companies registered with the Brazilian securities regulator and (2) survey of asset managers investing in Brazil.

Chapter 2 provides an overview of capital market trends and the investor landscape in Brazil. It includes trends in both initial and secondary equity public offerings, as well as activity in primary corporate bond markets. The chapter presents the shareholders of Brazilian listed companies and the ownership concentration at company level. It then offers a summary of recent developments in green bond issuance and Green House Gas (GHG) emissions markets.

Chapter 3 offers an overview of sustainability investing both globally and in Brazil. It includes trends in assets under management and key sustainability matters for institutional investors.

Chapter 4 summarises the most relevant characteristics of existing sustainability reporting frameworks and standards, and analyses their effective use by Brazilian public companies and disclosure preferences of asset managers investing in the country. The chapter then focuses on possible definitions of materiality, and how their advantages and drawbacks may be interpreted in the Brazilian context. It then considers the adoption of mandatory corporate sustainability disclosure and the choice of a single sustainability reporting standard in Brazil. Finally, the chapter analyses in detail data that may guide CVM and other institutions in prioritising which sustainability matters to concentrate their resources on.

Chapter 5 focusses on the quality of corporate disclosure. First, on the assurance of sustainability disclosure globally and in Brazil, and, second, on how sustainability matters may affect disclosure in financial statements and in other existing mandatory filings.

Chapter 6 introduces the key issues related to a corporation's purpose and to short-termism, and it also discusses the business case for sustainability considerations by the board of directors. The chapter also advances on the discussion about possible definitions of directors' fiduciary duties.

Chapter 7 assesses data and discussion on different forms of engagement between shareholders and public companies, including dialogue with directors, participation in shareholders' meetings and litigation. The chapter covers issues that are relevant to the exercise of shareholders rights both in traditional public companies and in companies with a clear mandate to fulfil sustainability goals.

The OECD Surveys on Sustainability Practices in Brazil

The research presented in this report is complemented by the findings from two OECD surveys on practices and views on corporate sustainability in Brazil:

- A survey of public companies registered with the Brazilian securities regulator (CVM);
- A survey of asset managers investing in Brazil.

While aggregated survey responses are presented in the following chapters as relevant, this section summarises the main characteristics of the respondents in both surveys.

Survey on Sustainability Practices of Public Companies in Brazil

CVM sent an online questionnaire hosted in an OECD webpage to all public companies in its registry in late November 2021 and respondents had until early January 2022 to fill the questionnaire. Most of these companies have listed shares (these are registered in category A), but a small minority is only allowed to make public offerings of debt securities (category B). The questionnaire was available in both English and Portuguese, and respondents were given the option to select their preferred language. The Brazilian Association of Public Companies (ABRASCA) also shared the link to the questionnaire in December 2021 with its associates. The efforts of both CVM and ABRASCA resulted in a high response rate to the survey. Sixty-three public companies with USD 489 billion of market capitalisation as of end 2020 answered to the questionnaire (7 of these do not currently have publicly traded equity).

The respondents' market capitalisation represented 49.5% of total market capitalisation in Brazil as of end 2020, and the industry distribution of respondents is broadly similar to the one of all public companies in Brazil with some overrepresentation of financials, energy and basic materials industries among respondents (see Figure 1.1 and Figure 2.1) Some bias in the group of respondents may be expected because companies with more advanced sustainability practices may be more prone to answer a survey on sustainability. However, due to the number of respondents and their industry distribution, as well as owing to the support to the survey from widely known institutions (ABRASCA, CVM and OECD), the group of respondents may be considered as representative of all Brazilian public companies.

Companies that answered the survey were divided into two groups. A first group with companies that are included in the most-often used large-cap index in Brazil (IBOVESPA) and another group with all other companies. IBOVESPA respondents had an average market capitalisation of USD 16.7 billion as of 2020, while the other respondents with listed equity had an average market value of USD 759 million. The segmentation of responses into two groups allows for a more nuanced view of the practices and perspectives according to distinct capabilities to comply with regulations and to answer investors' demands.

Figure 1.1. Profile of Respondents to the Survey on Sustainability Practices of Public Companies in Brazil

A. General summary of respondents

Number of companies	63
companies from IBOVESPA	28
others	35
Market capitalisation (USD billion)	489.4
IBOVESPA companies / all respondents	95%
Total market capitalisation in Brazil (USD billion)	988.4

B. Industry distribution, by market capitalisation

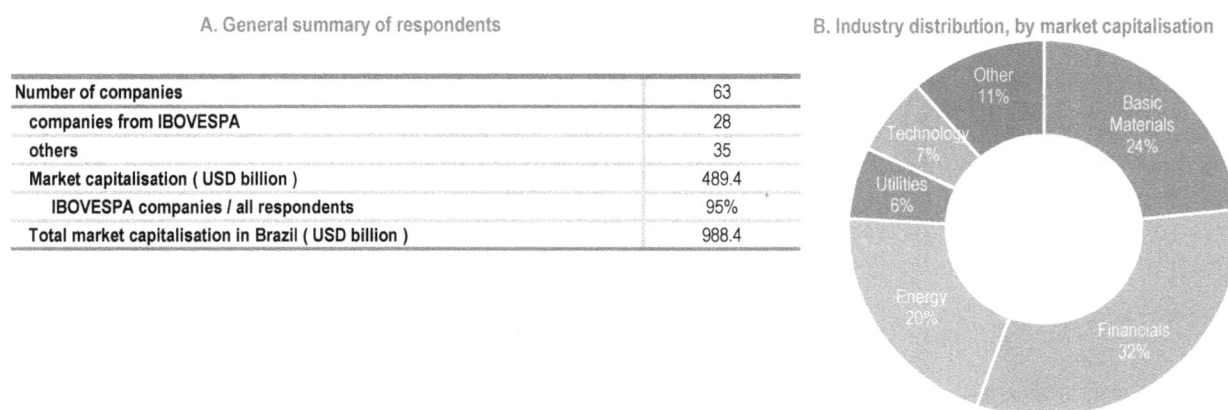

Notes:
1: Seven companies that responded to the survey do not currently have publicly traded equity. However, they are all registered as public companies with CVM and five of them have issued bonds in public markets.
2: IBOVESPA is Brazil's most-often used large-cap index, and it included 90 companies in early 2022.
3: Market capitalisation amounts are as of end 2020.
Source: OECD Survey on Sustainability Practices of Public Companies in Brazil, Thomson Reuters Datastream, World Federation of Exchanges.

Survey on Sustainability Practices of Asset Managers Investing in Brazil

As for the survey with investors, CVM sent an online questionnaire hosted in an OECD webpage to all asset managers ("administrador de carteira" in Portuguese) in its registry in late November 2021 and respondents had until early January 2022 to fill the questionnaire. These asset managers include mostly individual investment advisors and investment fund management firms ("gestores" in Portuguese), but also a small minority of administrators ("administrador fiduciário" in Portuguese). The questionnaire was available both in English and in Portuguese, and respondents were given the option to select their preferred language. The Brazilian Financial and Capital Markets Association (ANBIMA) also shared the link to the questionnaire in December 2021 with its associates. Likewise, the OECD contacted 17 asset managers headquartered outside of Brazil whose contact information was publicly available among the 50 asset managers with the biggest equity investments in the country as of end 2020.

The efforts of ANBIMA, CVM and OECD resulted in a very high response rate to the survey with 355 asset managers headquartered in Brazil and eight based abroad answering to the questionnaire. These asset managers declared to have USD 1 010 billion of assets under management (AUM) invested in Brazil in aggregate, including fixed income, alternative investments and equity (USD 981 of AUM for managers based in the country and USD 30 billion for the foreigners). There may be some double-counting in this total value of AUM because some asset managers may invest in funds managed by others and three respondents (with USD 10 billion of AUM) identified themselves as administrators. In any circumstance, the total AUM of respondents is very close to the USD 1 078 billion AUM of all investment funds managed by firms headquartered in Brazil as of end 2020 as reported by ANBIMA (2022[1]),[1] which demonstrates that the group of respondents represents a significant majority of asset managers headquartered in Brazil.

As mentioned in relation to the survey with public companies, some bias in the group of respondents may be expected because asset managers with more advanced sustainability practices may be more prone to answer a survey on sustainability. However, due to the considerably high number of respondents and the value of their AUM, the group of respondents may be considered as representative of all asset managers headquartered in Brazil. Specifically with respect to respondents' relevance for the public equity market, they had approximately USD 100 billion in equity investments as of end 2020, which represented 10.1% of total market capitalisation in Brazil.

Asset managers that answered to the survey were divided into three groups. Those with more than USD 1 billion of AUM are considered "large", the "medium" category includes those with AUM between USD 50 million and USD 1 billion, and "small" asset managers are those with less than USD 50 million of AUM. These thresholds were set with the goal of having most asset managers linked to financial conglomerates in the "large" category, and independent asset managers with the scale to invest in sophisticated technologies and human resources in the "medium" category. There are some highly qualified asset managers in the "small" category but it is a reasonable assumption that a majority of these may not have enough resources to analyse large amounts of information and engage with many companies.

Figure 1.2. Profile of Respondents to the Survey on Sustainability Practices of Asset Managers Investing in Brazil

A. By size

B. By portfolio distribution, share in total AUM

Note: "Large" asset managers are those with more than USD 1 billion of AUM, the "medium" category includes those with AUM between USD 50 million and USD 1 billion, and "small" asset managers are those with less than USD 50 million of AUM.
Source: OECD Survey on Sustainability Practices of Asset Managers Investing in Brazil.

References

ANBIMA (2022), *Estatísticas: Fundos de Investimento*, [1]
https://www.anbima.com.br/pt_br/informar/estatisticas/fundos-de-investimento/fundos-de-investimento.htm (accessed on 15 February 2022).

Note

[1] The comparison between the AUM of the respondents and the one of the investment fund industry as a whole, while relevant for the goals of this report, is not a perfect one for three reasons. First, OECD survey respondents may have considered assets managed on the basis of a simple mandate without the incorporation of an investment fund (a common practice for small portfolios). Second, respondents include eight managers incorporated abroad with USD 30 billion and six pension funds with USD 3 billion of AUM invested in Brazil. Third, ANBIMA's assessment includes investments abroad made by funds managed from Brazil, while the OECD questionnaire asked specifically for the "approximate value of the assets under […] management invested in Brazil".

2 Capital market trends and the investor landscape

This chapter first describes the equity market landscape in Brazil and selected countries. It provides an overview of the main trends in the use of equity markets with respect to both initial public offerings (IPOs) and secondary public offerings (SPOs) as well as delistings from the stock market. It also presents the ownership structure of listed companies in Brazil. The chapter then presents the corporate bond market landscape including green bonds in Brazil and in selected countries. The chapter ends with a summary of existing GHG emission markets.

Due to its long-term nature, equity financing contributes to innovation and long-term business dynamics, which are prerequisites for sustainable economic growth. Importantly, access to equity capital gives corporations the financial resilience that helps them overcome temporary downturns while still meeting their obligations to employees, creditors and suppliers. Additionally, the scrutiny by equity markets serves the critical function of redeploying capital from companies that have limited prospects for surviving to become long-term viable businesses. From the perspective of ordinary households, public equity markets provide an opportunity to directly or indirectly participate in corporate value creation and additional options for managing savings and plan for retirement.

The Brazilian public equity market

In 2007, the Bovespa Holding SA and the Brazilian Mercantile & Futures Exchange (BMF SA) merged and created the BM&FBOVESPA. In 2017, BM&FBOVESPA merged with CETIP and created the B3 – Brasil, Bolsa, Balcão. B3 provides trading services for securities listed on exchanges and trading on over the counter (OTC) markets. B3's scope of activities include the creation and management of trading systems, clearing, settlement, deposit and registration for the main classes of securities, from equities and corporate fixed income securities to currency and interest rate derivatives, securitisation products and agricultural commodities. B3 also acts as a central counterparty for most of the trades carried out in its markets and offers central depository and registration services. As a public company, shares issued by B3 are traded on its own stock exchange.

Currently, there are four listing segments in the B3 with different requirements designed to serve distinct company profiles, namely Novo Mercado, Level 1, Level 2 and Basic segments. In terms of corporate governance, Novo Mercado requires differentiated standards compared to the other listing segments such as the adoption of a set of corporate rules aimed at increasing minority shareholders' rights, as well as enhancing the disclosure of policies and the existence of monitoring and control structures. Among all segments of the B3, only Novo Mercado requires that companies establish an audit committee and disclose the following policies: (i) Compensation Policy; (ii) Nomination Policy of the Board of Directors, Advisory Committees and Executive Management Board; (iii) Risk Management Policy; (iv) Related Party Transaction Policy; and (v) Securities Trading Policy, with minimum requirements (except for the Compensation Policy).

Table 2.1. Requirements of the market segments in the B3

	Novo Mercado	Level 1	Level 2	Basic
Share Capital	Only common shares	Common and preferred shares (as per legislation)	Common and preferred shares (with additional rights)	Common and preferred shares (as per legislation)
Minimum percentage of outstanding share that can be traded by the general public (free float)	25% or 15% if the average daily trading volume is above BRL 25 million	25%	25%	There is no specific regulation
Composition of the Board of Directors	Minimum of 3 members, of which at least 2 or 20% (whichever is greater) must be independent with unified term of up to 2 years	Minimum of 3 members, with unified term of up to 2 years	Minimum of 5 members, of which at least 20% must be independent with unified term of up to 2 years	Minimum of 3 members (pursuant to Brazilian Corporations Law)
Board of Directors' duties	Statement on any public tender offer for the acquisition of shares issued by the company	There is no specific regulation	Statement on any public tender offer for the acquisition of shares issued by the company	There is no specific regulation
Audit Committee	Mandatory setting up of an audit committee or statutory audit committee	Optional	Optional	Optional
Financial Statements	As per legislation in force	As per legislation in force	Translated into English	As per legislation in force
Disclosure in English simultaneously with the disclosure in Portuguese	Material information and results press releases	There is no specific regulation	There is no specific regulation besides the financial statements	There is no specific regulation
Annual public shareholder meeting	Public meeting (in-person or by any other means that allow remote participation) must be hold until 5 business days after the disclosure of the quarterly and annual financial statements about the information disclosed	Mandatory (in-person)	Mandatory (in-person)	Optional

Source: B3 (2017[1]), Comparative list of segments, www.b3.com.br.

For the segments Level 1 and Level 2, companies are required to adopt specific practices. Level 1 companies largely try to improve methods of disclosure to the market participants and to increase the number of shareholders in their ownership structure. Level 2, in addition to the obligations of Level 1, requires that companies and its controlling shareholders must adopt and observe a much broader range of corporate governance practices and increase protection to minority shareholder rights (B3, 2022[2]). B3 also has the Basic segment that does not require additional corporate governance requirements beyond what is mandated by regulation.

As of 2021, there were 407 listed companies in the Brazilian public equity market with a total market capitalisation of USD 823.2 billion (Figure 2.1). Almost half of the companies are listed on Novo Mercado, and Level 1 and Level 2 companies together only represent 13% of the total number companies. With respect to the industry distribution of listed companies, financials, basic materials and consumer non-cyclicals are the top three industries accounting, respectively, for 22%, 16% and 13% of the total market capitalisation.

Figure 2.1. Summary statistics of the listed companies on B3 as of 2021

A. General summary

Number of companies	407
Novo Mercado	204
Level 1	28
Level 2	24
Basic	151
Total market capitalisation (USD billion)	823.2

B. Industry distribution, by market capitalisation

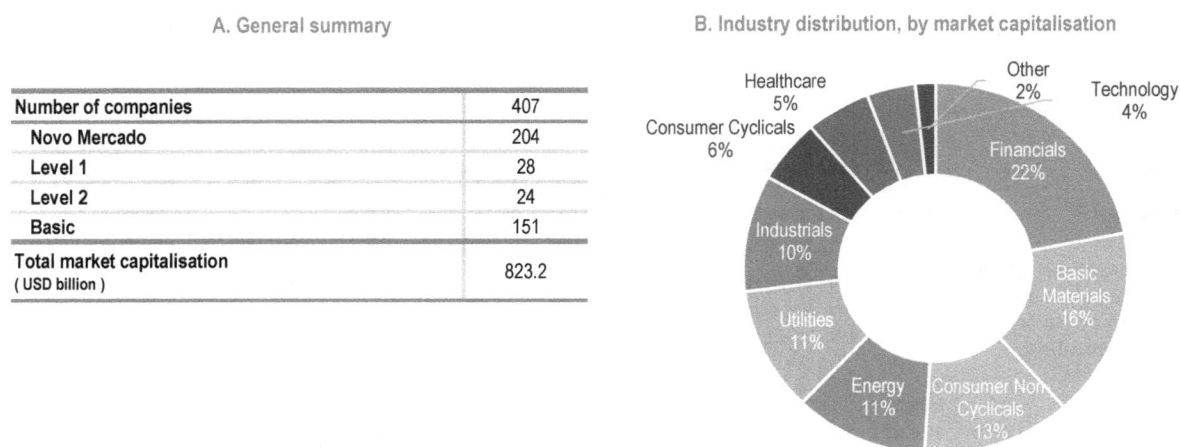

Note: Excluding investment funds and REITs.
Source: B3, Refinitiv.

Between 2000 and 2020, 190 new listings and 542 delistings have taken place in the Brazilian public equity market (Figure 2.2, Panel A). Net listings were only positive in 2007 and in 2020 when the Brazilian equity market saw a surge in listings. Total market capitalisation to GDP in Brazil was 68% as of end 2020, which is only higher than the one in Mexico among selected jurisdictions in Figure 2.2, Panel B. In the United States and in the United Kingdom, market capitalisation surpasses GDP. India, as many other Asian emerging markets, has experienced an increase in the use of public equity markets during the last two decades (OECD, 2022[3]).

Figure 2.2. Summary statistics of public equity market in Brazil

A. Newly listed and delisted companies in Brazil

B. Market capitalisation to GDP in Brazil and selected countries, as of 2020

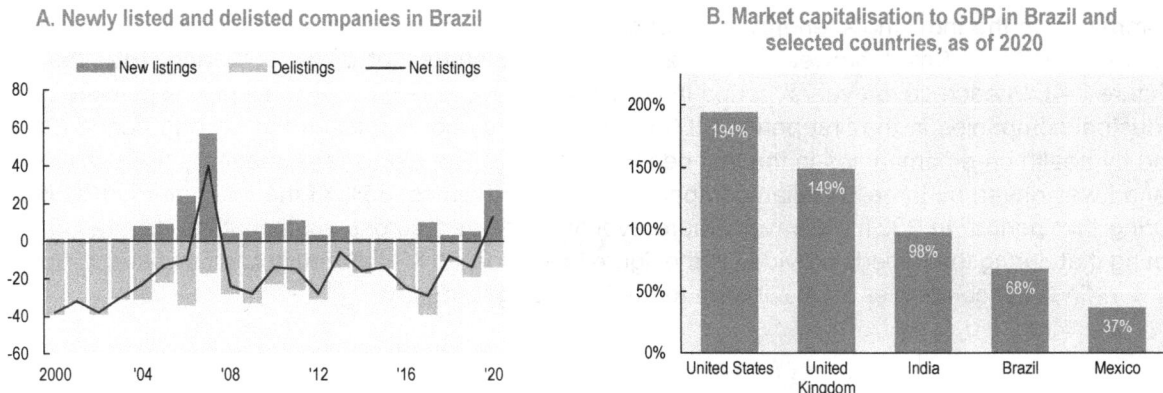

Note: In Panel A, investment funds and REITs are excluded. Market capitalisation in Panel B covers the domestic listed companies.
Source: OECD Capital Market Series Dataset, B3, Refinitiv, World Bank, World Federation of Exchanges.

Trends in initial public offerings

The Brazilian equity market has shown strong activity in initial public offerings (IPOs) in some periods since 2000. The annual number of companies joining the Brazilian public market together with the total amount of equity capital they raised is presented in Figure 2.3. IPO activity in Brazil reached its highest level in 2007, with a total of 57 companies raising almost USD 41 billion. Since 2008, the amount of equity raised decreased and has been on average USD 5 billion per year. However, the distribution of IPOs over time has been uneven and there was almost no activity in the market between 2014 and 2016. During the COVID-19 pandemic there has been a significant increase both in the number of IPOs and the amount of equity raised. Total proceeds raised in 2020 and 2021 via IPOs was approximately two and three times of the previous three-year average amount, respectively. In 2020 and 2021, a total of 69 companies raised equity capital through IPOs with a total amount of USD 19 billion.

Figure 2.3. Initial public offerings (IPOs) by companies in Brazil

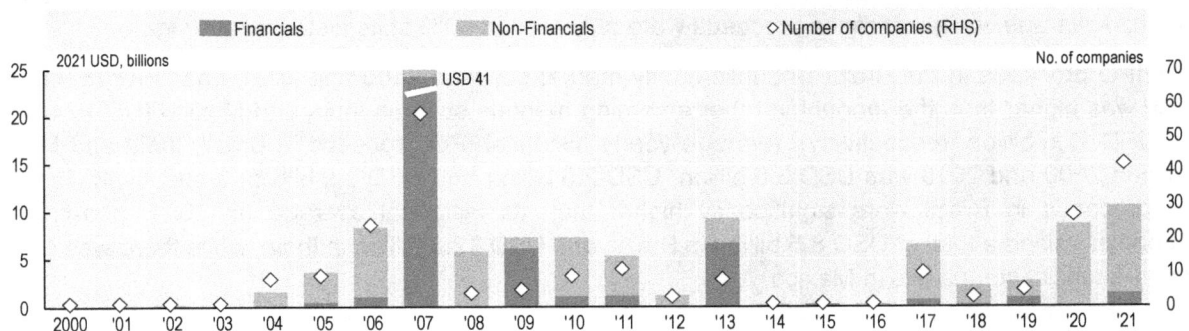

Source: OECD Capital Market Series Dataset, B3, see Annex for details.

Overall, the use of public equity markets by non-financial companies in Brazil has been lower compared to global levels. Between 2000 and 2021, the share of non-financial company IPO proceeds in Brazil was 63% of the total proceeds – including both financial and non-financial companies – while this number was

78% at the global level. Financial companies in Brazil raised the highest amount of equity in 2007 with USD 24 billion, which represents more than half of the proceeds raised between 2000 and 2021.

Companies in the industrials, energy and consumer-non-cyclicals industries dominated the non-financial company IPOs in Brazil between 2000 and 2021 with shares of 21%, 17% and 16% respectively (Figure 2.4). In each seven years' period in the figure below, at least 30% of all proceeds were raised by industrial companies in the first period (2000-06); by energy companies in the second period (2007-13); and by health care companies in the last period (2014-20). The high share of energy IPOs in the second period was driven by three Brazilian companies that raised almost 85% of the total energy IPO proceeds during that period. In 2021 IPOs were more evenly distributed across six industries. Overall, it is worth noting that during the periods provided in the figure below, only 5% of all equity capital raised through IPOs by non-financial companies in Brazil went to the technology industry.

Figure 2.4. Industry distribution of non-financial IPOs in Brazil, by total proceeds

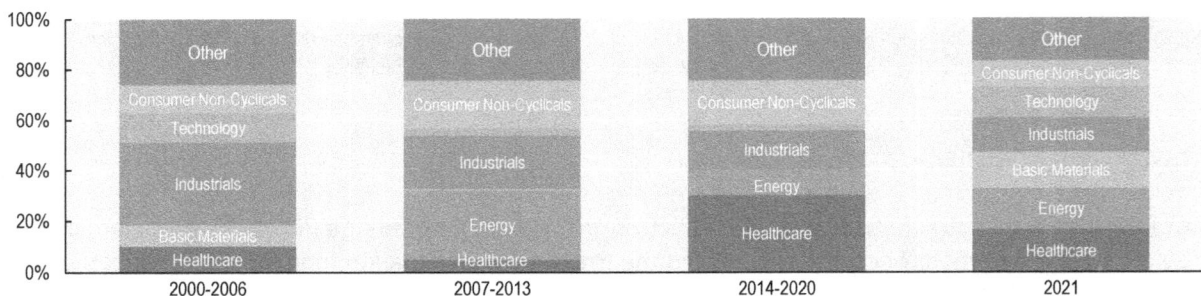

Source: OECD Capital Market Series Dataset, B3, see Annex for details.

Non-financial companies from the United States represent the highest share of total global IPO proceeds between 2000 and 2021. On average, almost 30% of all global IPO proceeds over that period was raised by US non-financial companies. Importantly, this share increased to 36% in 2020 and 2021. The average yearly IPO proceeds by non-financial company IPOs in the United States was USD 41 billion between 2000 and 2019 (Figure 2.5). Annual proceeds increased during the COVID-19 crisis, and they were significantly higher than the historical average, reaching USD 73 billion and USD 143 billion in 2020 and 2021, respectively. In the United Kingdom and France, IPO proceeds, after decreasing significantly in 2020, saw an increase in 2021. In the United Kingdom, proceeds in 2021 were 20% higher than the historical average, while in France proceeds were only around 60% of its historical average.

Total IPO proceeds in the Brazilian public equity market between 2000 and 2021 was USD 76.8 billion, which was higher than the amount in other emerging markets such as India and Mexico (USD 74 billion and USD 17.5 billion, respectively). Average yearly historical IPO proceeds in Brazil, India and Mexico between 2000 and 2019 was USD 3.5 billion, USD 2.9 billion and USD 0.9 billion, respectively. In 2020, IPO proceeds in Brazil were significantly higher than its historical average. In 2021, non-financial companies raised a total of USD 8.5 billion in Brazil, and USD 12.3 billion in India, while there was no IPO by non-financial companies in Mexico.

Figure 2.5. IPOs by non-financial companies in Brazil and selected countries

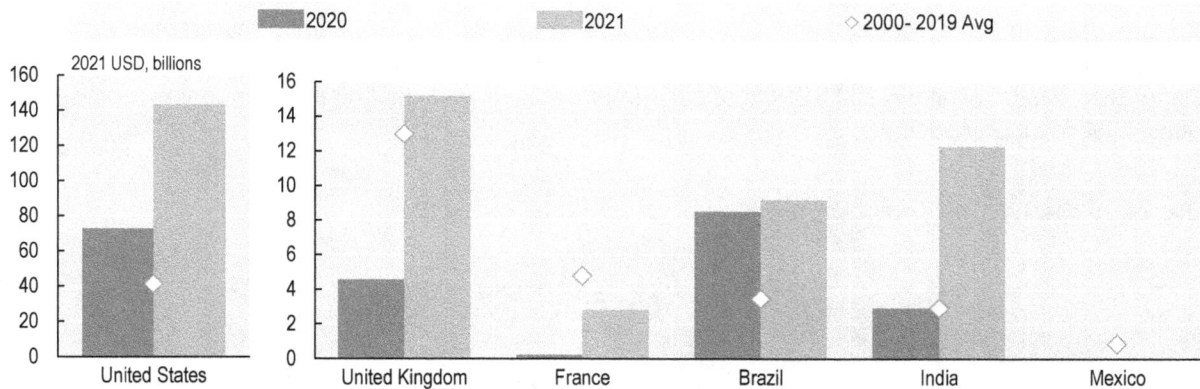

Source: OECD Capital Market Series Dataset, B3, see Annex for details.

Trends in secondary public offerings

Companies that are already listed on a stock exchange can raise additional equity on the primary public equity markets through secondary public offerings ("SPOs" or follow-on offerings). The proceeds from the SPOs may be used for a variety of purposes and can also help sound companies bridge a temporary downturn in economic activity. In this respect, SPOs played an important role in providing the corporate sector with capital in the wake of the 2008 financial crisis and through the 2020 during the COVID-19 crisis.

Since 2000, companies in Brazil have raised 2.5 times as much money through SPOs as they have raised through IPOs. In the wake of the 2008 global financial crisis, a record number of Brazilian listed companies in 2010 turned to the public equity market to raise a total of USD 100 billion through secondary offerings. Following the COVID-19 crisis, already listed companies in Brazil used public equity markets to a lesser extent when compared to the period following the 2008 global financial crisis. Globally, SPOs by financial companies represented an important share – almost one-third- between 2000 and 2021 – of all the total SPO proceeds. In Brazil, SPOs by financial companies only represented 12% of all SPOs between 2000 and 2021 (Figure 2.6).

Figure 2.6. Secondary public offerings (SPOs) by companies in Brazil

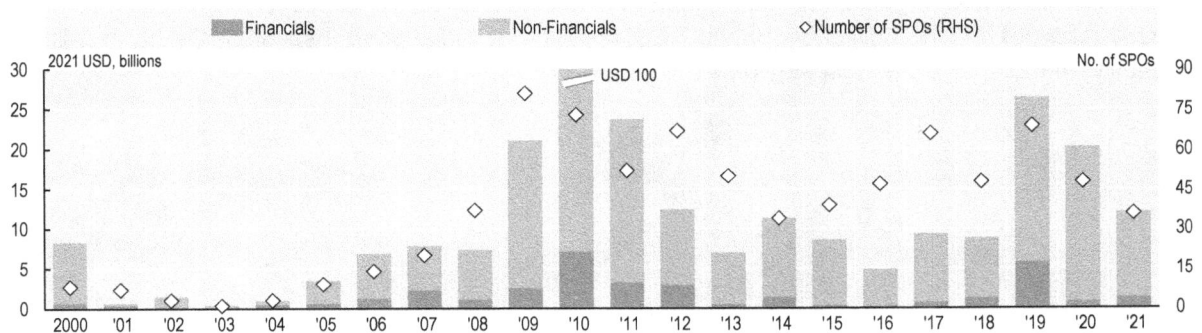

Source: OECD Capital Market Series Dataset, B3, see Annex for details.

Brazilian companies in the energy, consumer cyclicals and industrials industries were the top three industries by amount of capital raised in SPOs between 2000 and 2021 with corresponding shares of 35.7%, 13.4% and 10.4% respectively (Figure 2.7). Over the entire period, most of the energy industry SPOs took place in 2010, representing 75% of the total proceeds in 2010. During the first three periods presented in Figure 2.7the figure, health care and consumer cyclicals companies used comparatively fewer SPOs to raise capital, while in 2021 SPOs of consumer cyclicals and health care companies represented together 43% of all proceeds.

Figure 2.7. Industry distribution of SPOs in Brazil, by total proceeds

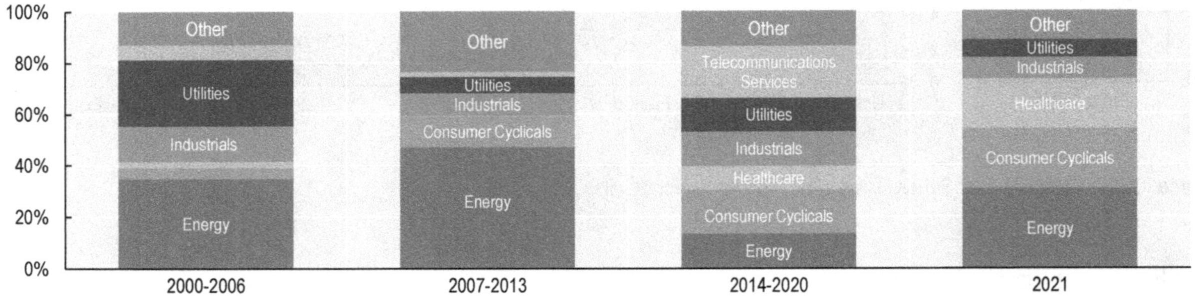

Source: OECD Capital Market Series Dataset, B3, see Annex for details.

As it is the case for IPOs, non-financial companies from the United States represented the highest share of total global SPO proceeds between 2000 and 2021. On average, around 30% of all the SPO proceeds between 2000 and 2021 was raised in the United States by non-financial companies. Between 2000 and 2019, the average yearly SPO proceeds of non-financial companies in Unites States was USD 114 billion and proceeds increased significantly following the COVID-19 pandemic (Figure 2.8). In 2020 and 2021, annual proceeds were significantly higher than their historical average between 2000 and 2019, reaching USD 219 billion and USD 169 billion respectively. In 2020 and 2021, non-financial listed companies raised less capital via SPOs in France compared to of the historical average between 2000 and 2019. In 2020, proceeds in the United Kingdom were 50% higher than its historical average. In 2021, use of SPOs in the UK by non-financial companies was slightly lower than its historical average.

Total SPO proceeds in the Brazilian public equity market between 2000 and 2021 was USD 268.5 billion, which was higher than the total in the Indian and Mexican markets (USD 203.8 billion and USD 17 billion, respectively). SPO proceeds in Brazil, India and Mexico by non-financial companies between 2000 and 2019 were on average USD 11.9 billion, USD 8.4 billion, and USD 0.9 billion, respectively. In 2020, SPO proceeds in Brazil were significantly higher than their historical average. In 2021, non-financial companies raised a total of USD 10.8 billion in Brazil, USD 14 billion in India, while use of SPOs by non-financial companies in Mexico was almost negligible.

Figure 2.8. SPOs by non-financial companies in Brazil and selected countries

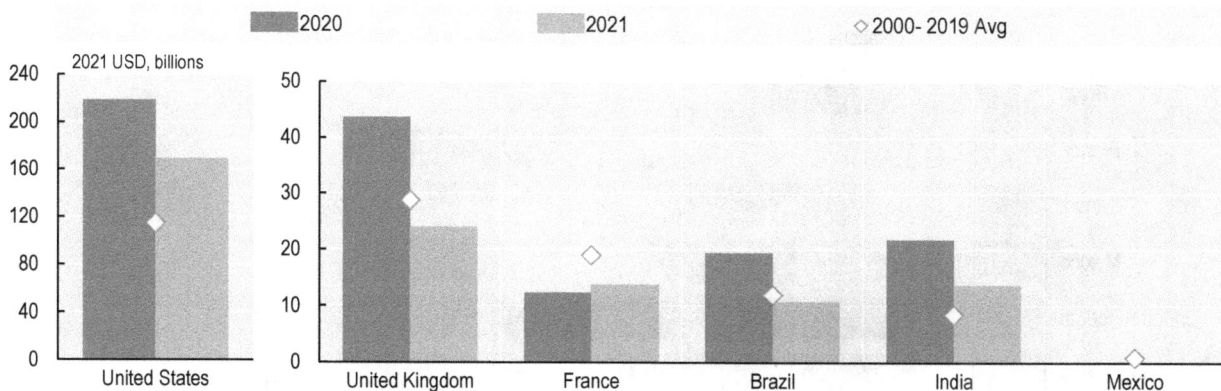

Source: OECD Capital Market Series Dataset, see Annex for details.

Investors and ownership structure in the Brazilian public equity market

To provide a complete picture of the Brazilian public equity market, it is important to understand the investor landscape and the ownership structure at the company level. Globally, ownership structures of the world's listed companies have experienced significant changes over the past two decades. One of the most important developments globally is the increase in institutional ownership (OECD, 2021[4]). However, there are important country and regional differences with respect to the different categories of investors that make up the largest shareholders at the company level.

Figure 2.9 shows the ownership distribution among different categories of owners in Brazil and selected countries, using the categories in (De La Cruz, Medina and Tang, 2019[5]), is provided in Figure 2.9. In both the United States and the United Kingdom, institutional owners are, by far, the largest category of owners holding 68% and 60% of the total capital, respectively. In France, institutional investors also rank first among different categories of investors with a comparatively lower share of the market capitalisation (27%). In Brazil and India, private corporations are the largest investor category, holding, respectively, 29% and 33% of total market capitalisation. Differently, strategic individuals rank first in Mexico as owners holding 34% of the listed equity, while in Brazil strategic individuals is the lowest among all categories holding only 8% of the listed equity. Among countries included in the figure below, public sector ownership, including the central and local governments and public pension funds, is the highest in India, representing the 12% of total market capitalisation, and followed by Brazil, representing a share of 10%.

Figure 2.9. Investor holdings at country level as of end-2020

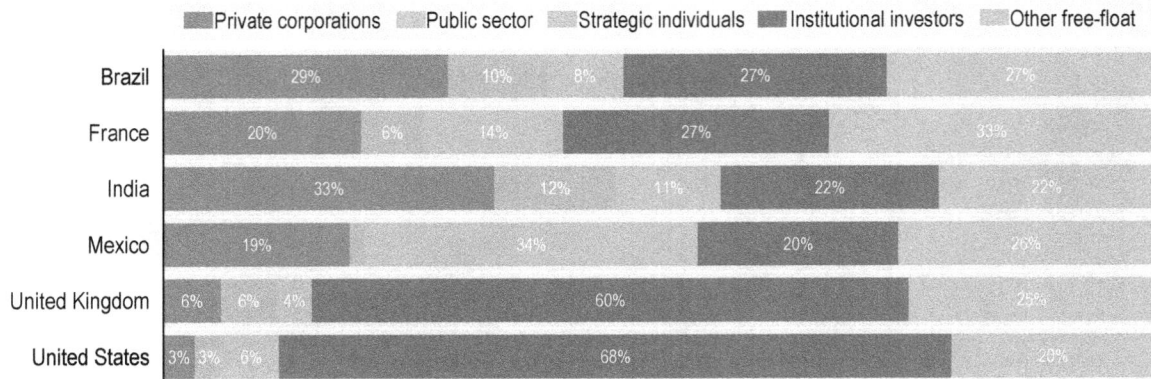

| | Private corporations | Public sector | Strategic individuals | Institutional investors | Other free-float |

Brazil	29%	10%	8%	27%	27%
France	20%	6%	14%	27%	33%
India	33%	12%	11%	22%	22%
Mexico	19%	34%	20%	26%	
United Kingdom	6%	6%	4%	60%	25%
United States	3%	3%	6%	68%	20%

Note: Other free-float refers to the holdings by shareholders that do not reach the threshold for mandatory disclosure of their ownership records or retail investors that are not required to do so.
Source: OECD Capital Market Series Dataset, Factset, Refinitiv, Bloomberg, see Annex for details.

Institutional investors can include a significant share of foreign ownership having further implications for the functioning of capital markets. The relative importance of domestic and foreign institutional investors in Brazil and selected countries is provided in Figure 2.10. While domestic institutional investors account for about 83% of all institutional investors' holdings in the United States, domestic institutional investors only account for 48% in the United Kingdom. In the US market, while domestic investors are dominant equity holders, in terms of total amount held foreign ownership is higher compared to all other markets. This is partly explained by the fact that the United States hosts many of the world's largest asset managers that also manage funds for non-US investors (De La Cruz, Medina and Tang, 2021[6]). France has the highest share of foreign institutional investors (77%). Similarly, in Mexico, Brazil and India, the institutional investor landscape is dominated by foreign investors who hold 67%, 65% and 61% of all institutional investors, respectively.

Figure 2.10. Domestic and foreign institutional ownership in Brazil and selected countries, as of end 2020

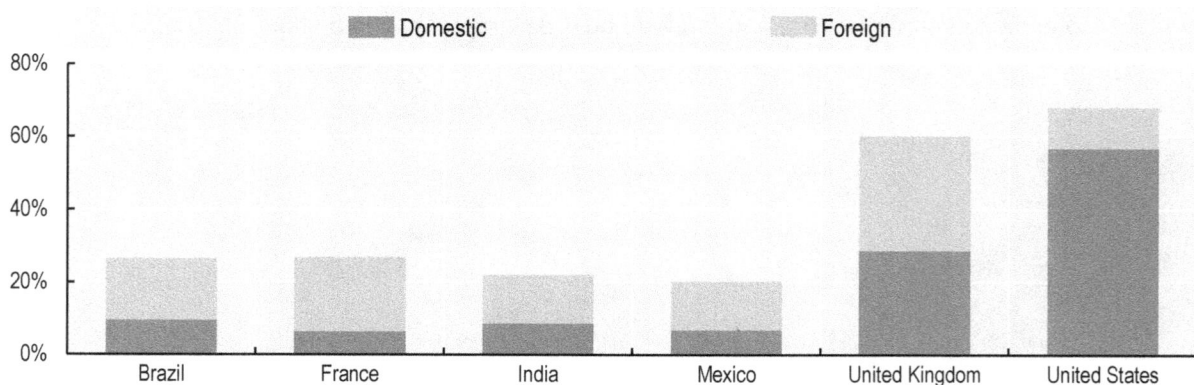

Source: OECD Capital Market Series Dataset, Factset, Refinitiv, Bloomberg, see Annex for details.

Increasing ownership concentration has been documented by the OECD work as a common phenomenon across markets. However, there are important differences with respect to the categories of owners that make up the largest owners and how this could affect the design of corporate governance regulations. The degree of concentration and control by individual shareholders at the company level is notably relevant for the regulation of related party transactions, takeovers and other matters related to the relationship between controlling and non-controlling shareholders (OECD, 2021[4]). Table 2.2 shows the average combined holdings of the largest shareholders in the listed corporate sector in Brazil and selected countries.

In Brazil ownership concentration is also a common characteristic in listed companies. The average combined holdings of the top three investors is 56.7%, close to the levels in France, India and Mexico. This high concentration is mainly the result of significant ownership by private corporations as the top three private corporations own on average 23% of the equity in each company in Brazil. This may be seen as an indication of strong presence of company group structures. The top three strategic individual investors and institutional investors have an average combined holding of 15% and 11% respectively.

Table 2.2. Ownership concentration at company level in Brazil and selected countries, as of end 2020

	Largest 1	Largest 3	Largest 5	Largest 20	Largest 50
Brazil	**40.6%**	**56.7%**	**62.2%**	**71.3%**	**73.2%**
France	42.3%	55.9%	60.7%	68.7%	71.0%
India	37.6%	54.0%	60.9%	72.6%	73.9%
Mexico	44.9%	56.6%	60.8%	67.0%	68.4%
United Kingdom	19.7%	36.3%	45.1%	64.6%	69.8%
United States	18.5%	33.0%	41.1%	60.5%	68.9%

Source: OECD Capital Market Series Dataset, Factset, Refinitv, Bloomberg, see Annex for details.

One important long-term trend in the public equity markets globally has been the growing use of index investment strategies by institutional investors. This trend has resulted in a significant difference with respect to institutional ownership between companies included in major indices and those that are not. In addition, because most indices weight companies according to their market capitalisation and free-float levels, being a large corporation with higher free-float, all else equal, will result in a higher weighting in the index. Against this background, companies included in the MSCI indices found to have a higher average institutional ownership than non-index companies. For instance, companies that are included in the MSCI Emerging Markets Index have on average 16% institutional holdings compared to 7% for companies that are not included (OECD, 2021[7]).

This trend also holds for the Brazilian companies that are included in the MSCI Emerging Markets and MSCI Emerging Markets ESG Leaders[1] indices. As of September 2021, there were, respectively, 49 and 26 Brazilian companies with total market capitalisation of USD 740 billion and USD 322 billion. Brazilian companies in MSCI EM index have on average 27% institutional holdings compared to 23% for Brazilian companies that are not included in the index (Figure 2.11, Panel A). Brazilian companies in MSCI EM ESG Leaders index have on average 29% institutional holdings compared to 23% for Brazilian companies that are not included in the index. Of special relevance, Brazilian companies correspond to a share of 4.6% of the MSCI EM index, but only to a share of 2.8% of the MSCI EM ESG Leaders index.

Comparison of industry distribution between all Brazilian listed companies and index included Brazilian companies reveal that companies from financials and industrials industries correspond more than 50% of the market capitalisation of the companies included in the MSCI EM ESG Leaders index. Financials, basic materials and consumer non-cyclicals together dominate the listed company and MSCI EM index company universe for Brazil (Figure 2.11, Panel B).

Figure 2.11. Institutional investors' holdings in index companies versus non-index companies in Brazil (as of end-2020)

A. Institutional investors' holdings in index companies

B. Industry distribution of listed companies and index companies in Brazil

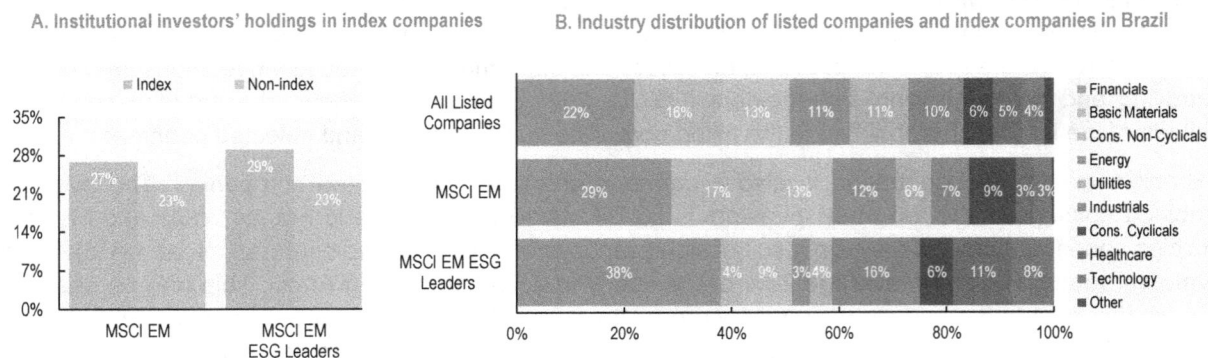

Note: Listed companies in Brazil do not include investment funds and REITs. The information on MSCI constituents is as of end 2020.
Source: OECD Capital Market Series dataset, FactSet, Refinitiv, Bloomberg, B3, MSCI Constituents Information.

Trends in corporate bond issuances

Compared to ordinary bank loans, corporate bonds typically have longer maturities. In addition, the absence or relatively limited requirements for collateral gives corporate bond financing a special role as a source of financing compared to other types of borrowing. In the aftermath of the 2008 global financial crisis, there has been a significant and lasting increase in corporate bond issuances worldwide. Annual corporate bond issuances by non-financial companies doubled from an average of USD 932 billion between 2000 and 2007 to an average of almost USD 2 trillion between 2008 and 2021.[2] Corporate bonds have also become an increasingly important source of finance for Brazilian companies. The annual number of Brazilian companies that raised funds via corporate bonds between 2000 and 2021 together with the total amount of capital raised are presented in Figure 2.12. Overall, between 2000 and 2021, Brazilian companies raised a total of USD 864 billion in bonds, with 60% of this amount raised by non-financial companies. Corporate bond issuances reached its highest level in 2010, with a total of 168 Brazilian companies raising USD 87 billion. The activity was relatively high between 2010 and 2014, when the annual average issuances were USD 74 billion. Since 2015, annual issuances saw a decline, averaging only USD 33 billion.

Figure 2.12. Corporate bond issuances by Brazilian companies

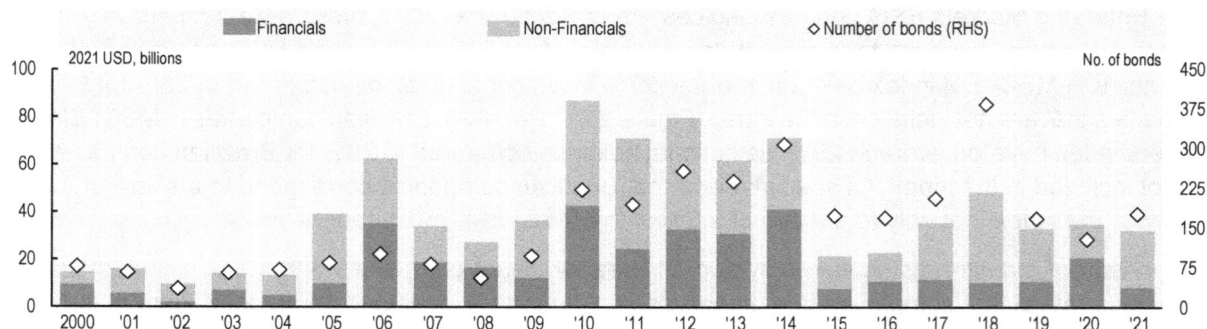

Source: OECD Capital Market Series Dataset, Refinitiv, see Annex for details.

Industrials, utilities and basic materials were the top three industries by the amount of capital raised between 2000 and 2021 in Brazil, with a share of 24%, 23% and 14%, respectively (Figure 2.13). Three industries, namely industrials, utilities, and consumer non-cyclicals, experienced an increase in the amount raised from 58% of the total proceeds raised between 2000 and 2006, to 67% of the total proceeds in 2021.

Figure 2.13. Industry distribution of corporate bonds by Brazilian companies, by total proceeds

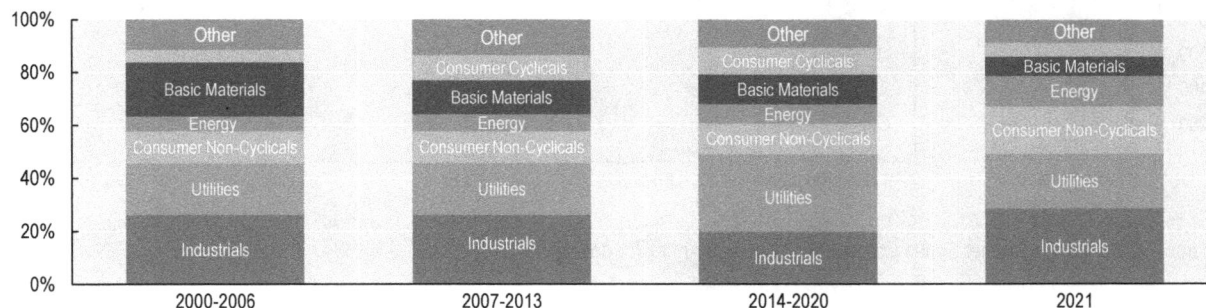

Source: OECD Capital Market Series Dataset, Refinitiv, see Annex for details.

Non-financial companies from the United States are the largest users of corporate bonds globally. Forty-two percent of all corporate bond proceeds between 2000 and 2021 was raised by US non-financial companies. Annual proceeds of US non-financial companies increased significantly following the start of the COVID-19 crisis. Indeed, it was significantly higher than its historical average (2000-19) reaching USD 1.4 trillion and USD 918 billion in 2020 and 2021, respectively (Figure 2.14). In the United Kingdom and France, 2020 proceeds surpassed their historical average. However, in 2021 the total amount raised by UK and French companies decreased. In the United Kingdom, proceeds were 71% of the historical average, while they were slightly lower than its historical average in France.

Over the 2000-21 period, Brazilian non-financial companies raised more funds via corporate bonds than Indian and Mexican non-financial companies. The total amount of capital raised via corporate bonds by Brazilian, Mexican and Indian non-financial companies was USD 489 billion, USD 444 billion and USD 260 billion respectively. In 2020, corporate bond issuances by Brazilian companies decreased and was lower than the historical average. In 2021, however, total amount raised was in line with the historical average. Indian and Mexican non-financial companies increased their use of corporate bonds in 2020 compared to their historical averages. In 2021, corporate bond issuances by Indian and Mexican companies were still above historical averages.

Bonds issued at longer maturities may be particularly helpful for companies in times of financial distress as they help extending the debt obligations of the company. In this respect, the average maturity of corporate bonds at origination indicates, on average, for how long a company with liquidity problems can sustain the pressure of refinancing its debt. Globally, there has been an increase in average maturities of corporate bonds issued by non-financial companies, with the increase being most pronounced for investment grade companies that extended maturities from eight years in 2000 to 13.4 years in 2021. However, across countries and regions, average maturities for corporate bonds issued by non-financial companies vary widely.

Figure 2.14. Bond issuance by non-financial companies from Brazil and selected countries

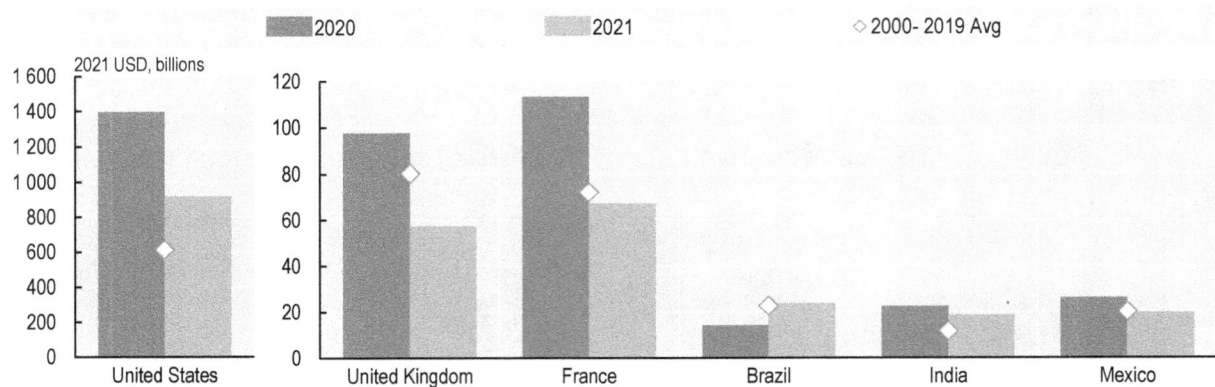

Source: OECD Capital Market Series Dataset, Refinitiv, see Annex for details.

Average maturities for corporate bonds by non-financial companies from Brazil and selected countries for the 5-year periods of 2000-04 and 2017-21 are presented in Figure 2.15. Over the periods provided in the figure below, the United States, the United Kingdom, France and Mexico have seen substantial increases in average maturities. While the increase in average maturities for Brazilian non-financial corporate bonds were comparatively low, average maturities in India experienced a slight decline. Among the six countries shown in the figure, Brazil had the lowest average maturity for corporate bonds in 2021 (6.6 years) while the United Kingdom had the highest maturity (14 years).

Figure 2.15. Average maturities for corporate bonds by non-financial companies from Brazil and selected countries

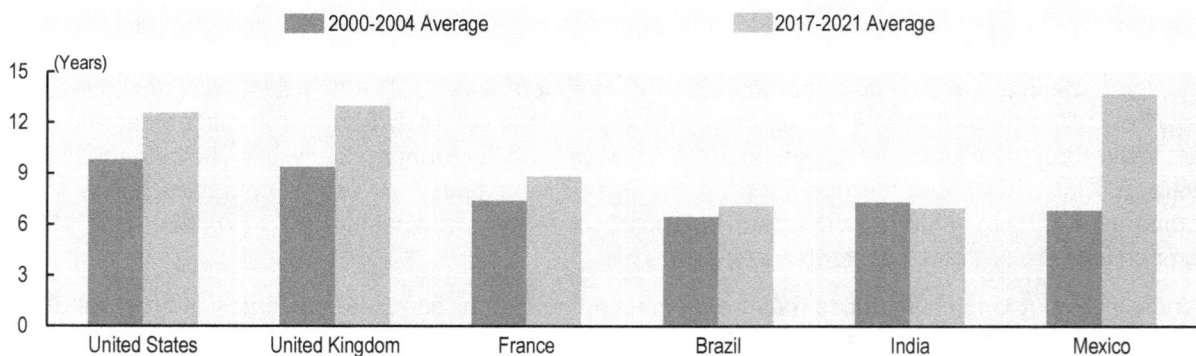

Note: Maturity is the average of the original maturity equally weighted proceeds. Over the period 2017-21, total number of corporate bonds issued by Mexican companies is the lowest by number, however, Mexcio has a higher share of corporate bonds having maturity more than 15 years to total corpoate bonds compared to other countries. This leads to higher average maturity for Mexico during this period.
Source: OECD Capital Market Series Dataset, Refinitiv, see Annex for details.

Green bonds and other ESG bonds

According to one estimate, a USD 6.9 trillion investment between 2015 and 2030 would be needed to meet climate objectives in the infrastructure industry only in line with the Paris Agreement (OECD, 2017[8]). Another estimate related to the energy industry claims that annual clean energy investment worldwide will need to more than triple by 2030 to around USD 4 trillion to reach net-zero emissions by 2050 (IEA, 2021[9]). At the regional level, for example, financing the net-zero GHG emissions target of the EU by 2050 is estimated to cost an annual investment of 2% of GDP (Darvas and Wolff, 2021[10]).

Public resources alone will not be enough to cover the trillions of dollars needed to fulfil the goals of the Paris Agreement, and to adapt infrastructure and industrial systems to climate change. Private financing sources such as institutional investors will also have a key role to play in financing the climate transition. Recently, green bonds have been issued as an alternative financing instruments in relation to the climate change. The criteria for determining whether an activity financed by the issuance of a corporate bond is environmentally sustainable, however, can vary. In order to protect the buyers of corporate bonds and other financial instruments, some jurisdictions have been developing a taxonomy to classify which economic activities could be considered environmentally sustainable (allowing, for instance, a company to name a bond it issues as "green").[3]

There has been a gradual increase in the amount of funds raised via green bonds, reaching almost USD 560.4 billion in 2021 (Figure 2.16, Panel A), with 67% of this amount (USD 378.1 billion) issued by corporations, and the rest is issued by others, including agencies, governments, central banks, supranational institutions and municipalities. Still these amounts are modest compared to the USD 19.1 trillion of government borrowing by OECD countries (OECD, 2022[11]) as well as the USD 5.8 trillion in corporate bond borrowing for the same year.[4]

Overall, between 2000 and 2021, there were 35 issuers of green bonds in Brazil, among which 23 are either listed or subsidiaries of listed companies. In 2019, issuances in Brazil saw a surge, when 43 green corporate bonds were issued with total proceeds of USD 3.9 billion (Figure 2.16).

Figure 2.16. Green bond issuances, by issuer type and number

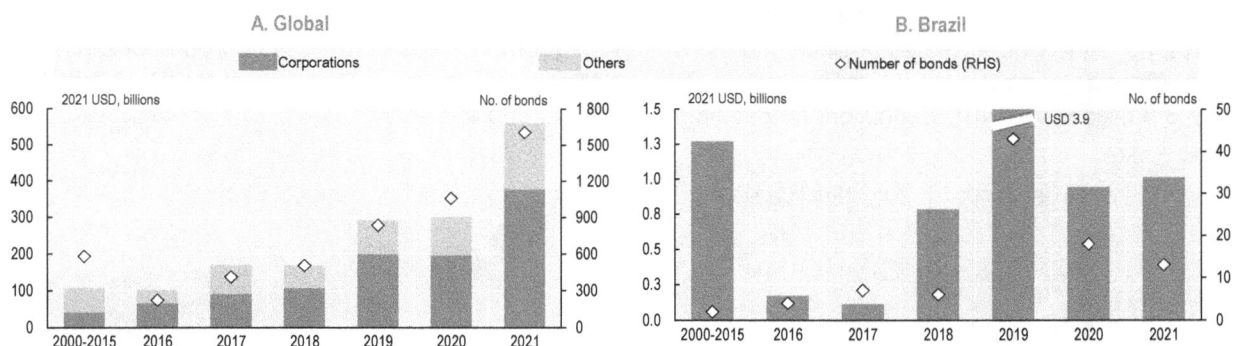

Note: Others include agencies, governments, treasuries, central banks, supranational, and non-US municipalities.
Source: Refinitiv, B3, see Annex for details.

Global industry distribution of green bonds' issuers reveals that the financial industry accounts for half of the total funds raised between 2000 and 2021 (Figure 2.17, Panel A). Government activity, utilities, and industrials followed financials with shares of 16%, 13% and 9% of the total proceeds. In Brazil, the utilities industry dominates the green bond issuances with 75% of all the green bond issuances (Figure 2.17, Panel B). Different from the global picture, in Brazil the financial industry represents a modest share of green bonds (9%).

Figure 2.17. Industry composition of green bonds between 2000 and 2021

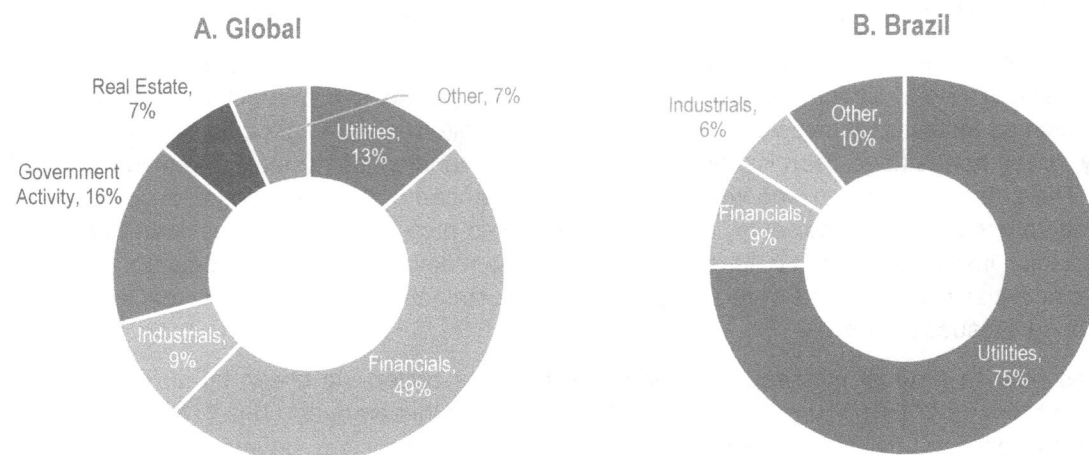

A. Global

B. Brazil

Note: This figure includes information on bonds issued by corporations, agencies, governments, central banks, supranational institutions and municipalities.
Source: Refinitiv, B3, see Annex for details.

As seen in Figure 2.18, issuers domiciled in France and in the United States raised USD 193.4 billion and USD 183.3 of funds, respectively, via green bonds between 2000 and 2021. Corporations in the United States represented a higher share of the total green bonds issued by both corporations and governments when compared to the share of corporations in France. The total amount of funds raised via green bonds by issuers in the United Kingdom was USD 64.4 billion between 2000 and 2021, and 55% of the funds were raised by corporations. Green bond issuances in Mexico, India and Brazil were modest compared to the United States, France and the United Kingdom. Issuers were mostly corporations in those three emerging markets, and total funds raised in Mexico, India, and Brazil were USD 10.1 billion, USD 8.8 billion, and USD 8.2 billion, respectively, between 2000 and 2021.

Figure 2.18. Green bond issuances from Brazil and selected countries between 2000-21

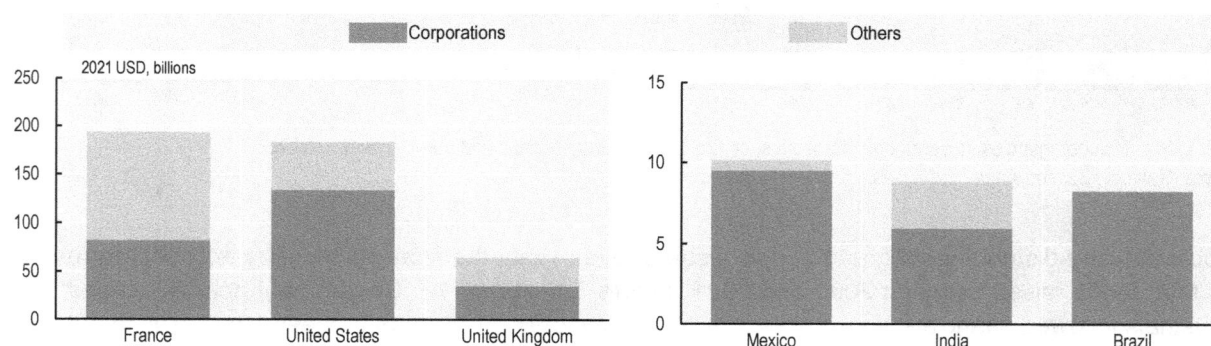

Note: Others include agencies, governments, treasuries, central banks, supranational, and municipalities.
Source: Refinitiv, B3, see Annex for details.

Green bonds are usually defined as bonds whose proceeds are used to invest in a portfolio of projects with positive environmental results. There are two other similar bonds, which are named "social bonds" if their proceeds should be directed to projects with positive social results and "sustainability bonds" in case the portfolio of projects aims at both environmental and social positive impacts. There is, however, another category called "sustainability-linked bonds" (SLB) whose proceeds may be used for general corporate purpose, and not specifically for a portfolio of projects (ICMA, 2020[12]). In SLBs, the characteristics of the bonds (usually the interest rate paid to the bond) vary according to the sustainability performance of the company. Typically, the company needs to pay a higher coupon if it did not reach a predefined sustainability performance target.

Globally, the amount of funds raised via sustainability, social and sustainability-linked bonds increased significantly to USD 472 billion in 2021 from USD 81 billion in 2019 and USD 28 billion in 2018.[5] The share of corporations in total amount of funds raised between 2018 and 2021 was on average one-third of the yearly issued funds. In Brazil, first sustainability-linked bond issued in 2020,[6] and then there have been five social bonds and two more sustainability-linked bonds issued during the last two years. Total amount of funds raised of these bonds was USD 3.7 billion.

GHG emissions markets

Limiting global warming to 1.5°C above pre-industrial levels would effectively require CO_2 emissions to decline by about 45% from 2010 levels by 2030 and reach net zero emissions around 2050 (IPCC, 2018[13]). So far, 165 jurisdictions have presented a national plan (named as nationally determined contribution) on how they will reduce GHG emissions in line with the Paris Agreement (so-called "national determined contributions"). However, total global GHG emissions level in the existing nationally determined contributions of Parties to the Paris Agreement by 2030 is still projected to be 15.9% higher than in 2010 and 4.7% higher than in 2019 (UN, 2021[14]). In this respect, with a view to increase the efforts towards net zero emissions, during COP26 in November 2021, governments agreed on the Glasgow Climate Pact to accelerate action on coal, deforestation, electric vehicles and methane, and they finalised the outstanding elements of the Paris Agreement, including the establishment of a new mechanism and standards for international carbon markets (UN, 2021[15]).

Table 2.3. Summary of national and regional emission trading systems

	EU ETS	NZ ETS	RGGI	WCI	SK ETS	China ETS	UK ETS
Start date	2005	2008	2009	2013	2015	2021	2021
Percent economy-wide emissions covered by ETS	~40%	~50%	~10%	California: 75% Quebec: 78%	~75%	~40%(*)	~10%
2030 reduction target	At least 55%	30%	30%	California: 40%. Quebec: 37.5%	24.4%	65%	68%
Reduction target on	GHG Levels	GHG Levels	GHG Levels	GHG Levels	GHG Levels	CO2 emissions per unit of GDP	GHG Levels
Base year for reduction target	1990	2005	2020	1990	2017	2005	1990
Total market value of ETS in 2021 (EUR million)	682 501	2 505	49 260		798	1 289	22 847

Note: (*) For power sector only, gradually expanding to 75% during 2021-25 of sectors including petrochemical, chemical, building materials, steel, nonferrous metals, paper, and domestic aviation.
Source: Refinitiv.

In terms of carbon trading, the finalisation of the Paris Agreement's Article 6 during COP26 text was an important outcome that sets the rules for how countries may use trading to help achieve their national climate targets and affects how firms will seek to achieve corporate carbon reduction targets. The final rules include safeguards to prevent "double counting" of emission reductions. Article 6 creates a unit called an Internationally Traded Mitigation Outcome (ITMO) representing an amount of reduced or avoided emissions, which by definition requires the seller country to deduct that amount of emission reduction in terms of reaching its declared national climate target. These accounting requirements, which are called "corresponding adjustments", ensure that each unit of emission reduction is only considered as a credit by the party that paid for it.

There has been a gradual increase in the traded value of the emission trading systems (ETSs) with a significant expansion in 2021. The traded value in 2021 reached EUR 760 billion, which was 2.5 times the value traded in the previous year (Figure 2.19, Panel A). In 2021, the European ETS had the highest share traded value and volume among the seven major ETSs provided in Table 2.3 (see Figure 2.19, Panels B and C). Introduced in July 2021, the People's Republic of China (China)'s national ETS had a market value at around EUR 1.3 billion as of end 2021. Brazil does not currently have an emissions trading system, but a bill of law that would regulate such a market ("Projeto de Lei n. 528/21") has been approved by all relevant commissions in Congress' Lower Chamber.

Figure 2.19. Summary statistics of emission trading systems

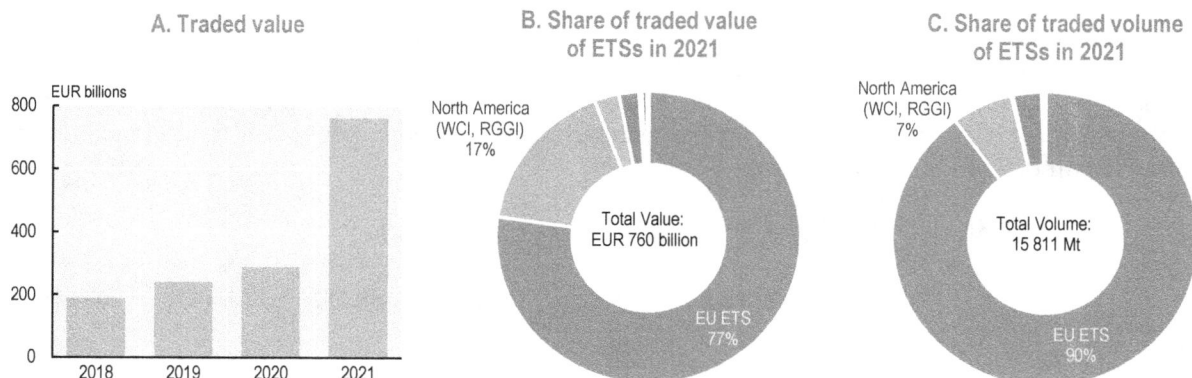

A. Traded value
B. Share of traded value of ETSs in 2021
C. Share of traded volume of ETSs in 2021

Notes:
1: Amounts include the EU ETS, the UK ETS, from North America the WCI, RGGI, and the emerging market in Mexico, in China the regional pilot ETS, offset trading (CCERs) and the national China ETS, from Korea (SK ETS), from New Zealand, NZ ETS, and an assessment of what is left of global offset transactions from the old Clean Development Mechanism (CDM) market.
2: For the EU ETS, traded volume and value include spot, auctions and futures, but option positions are not included. For China, traded volume includes allowance units for pilot ETS, national ETS (for 2021), and CCER transactions, and traded value includes only allowances.
Source: Refinitiv.

Voluntary carbon credit markets allow entities not covered by ETS to manage their carbon footprint or to raise private financing for projects with positive contributions for the climate transition (TSVCM, 2021[16]). In the case when a company with a self-imposed target of net-zero emissions, it can acquire carbon credits sold in these markets. For a system of carbon credits or permits to work efficiently, however, the certification of emissions reduction and carbon captured must be credible (just like external auditors and custodians are needed for a stock market to flourish) and flows of negotiation should be as free as feasible (so that carbon emission's reductions are achieved for the smallest possible costs). Standardisation of carbon credits is especially important to facilitate trading flows, cross-border negotiations and price-discovery.

The voluntary carbon markets are still evolving. In general, transactions of offsets in the voluntary carbon markets take place "over the counter" (OTC) on a bilateral basis. Since only a limited share of total voluntary carbon market transactions takes place on exchanges, there is no source for aggregated traded volumes and prices. However, during 2021, companies increasingly preferred centralised marketplaces than the OTC (Refinitiv, 2021[17]). Total traded value in centralised voluntary carbon markets reached its annual peak value in early November 2021 with USD 1 billion. Total traded volume between January and November 2021 also reached to almost 300 million tonnes, which represents a significant increase from 188 million tonnes in 2020 and 104 million tonnes in 2019. This has been reflected by the increase in the average volume-weighted price of offsets: from USD 2.5 per tonne in 2020 to USD 3.5 per tonne in 2021 (Refinitiv, 2021[17]).

References

B3 (2022), *Listing segments*, https://www.b3.com.br/en_us/products-and-services/solutions-for-issuers/listing-segments/nivel2/. [2]

B3 (2017), *Comparative list of segments*. [1]

Darvas, Z. and G. Wolff (2021), *A green fiscal pact: climate investment in times of budget consolidation*. [10]

De La Cruz, A., A. Medina and Y. Tang (2021), "Institutional ownership in today's equity markets", *(Forthcoming)*. [6]

De La Cruz, A., A. Medina and Y. Tang (2019), "Owners of the World's Listed Companies", *OECD Capital Market Series, Paris*, http://www.oecd.org/corporate/Owners-of-the-Worlds-Listed-Companies.htm. [5]

ICMA (2020), *Sustainability-Linked Bond Principles*, https://www.icmagroup.org/assets/documents/Regulatory/Green-Bonds/June-2020/Sustainability-Linked-Bond-Principles-June-2020-171120.pdf. [12]

IEA (2021), *Net Zero 2050: A Roadmap for the Global Energy Sector*, https://iea.blob.core.windows.net/assets/beceb956-0dcf-4d73-89fe-1310e3046d68/NetZeroby2050-ARoadmapfortheGlobalEnergySector_CORR.pdf. [9]

IPCC, I. (2018), *Global warming of 1.5°C: Summary for Policymakers*, https://www.ipcc.ch/. [13]

OECD (2022), "Corporate Finance in Asia and the COVID-19 Crisis", *OECD Capital Market Series*, http://www.oecd.org/corporate/asia/corporate-finance-in-asia-and-the-covid-19-crisis.htm. [3]

OECD (2022), *OECD Sovereign Borrowing Outlook 2022*, OECD Publishing, Paris, https://doi.org/10.1787/b2d85ea7-en. [11]

OECD (2021), *Background Note on Institutional Investor Ownership in Latin American Equity Markets*, https://www.oecd.org/corporate/ca/Institutional-investors-background-note-Latin%20America-2021.pdf. [7]

OECD (2021), *The Future of Corporate Governance in Capital Markets Following the COVID-19 Crisis*, OECD Publishing, Paris, https://doi.org/10.1787/efb2013c-en. [4]

OECD (2017), *Investing in Climate, Investing in Growth*, OECD Publishing, Paris, https://doi.org/10.1787/9789264273528-en. [8]

Refinitiv (2021), *Carbon Market Year in Review 2021*. [17]

TSVCM (2021), *Taskforce on Scaling Voluntary Carbon Markets - Final Report*, https://www.iif.com/tsvcm. [16]

UN (2021), *Nationally determined contributions under the Paris Agreement*, https://unfccc.int/process-and-meetings/the-paris-agreement/nationally-determined-contributions-ndcs/nationally-determined-contributions-ndcs/ndc-synthesis-report#eq-5 (accessed on 20 December 2021). [14]

UN (2021), *The Glasgow Climate Pact – Key Outcomes from COP26*, https://ukcop26.org/wp-content/uploads/2021/11/COP26-Presidency-Outcomes-The-Climate-Pact.pdf. [15]

Notes

[1] The MSCI Emerging Markets (EM) ESG Leaders Index is a capitalisation weighted index that provides exposure to companies with high ESG performance relative to their sector peers. MSCI EM ESG Leaders Index consists of large and mid-cap companies across 24 EM economies.

[2] OECD Capital Market Series Dataset.

[3] See, for instance, Regulation EU 2020/852 on the establishment of a framework to facilitate sustainable investment.

[4] OECD Capital Market Series Dataset.

[5] Refinitiv, see Annex for details

[6] In September and November 2020, Suzano Austria issued a sustainability-linked bond in Brazil raising two separate proceeds of USD 750 million and USD 500 million, respectively. The bonds have KPIs aimed to reduce GHG emissions of the company by 2025 and if the company does not fulfil this sustainability performance target, the interest rate payable on the bonds will increase by 25 basis points from 2026 until the maturity of the bond in 2031.

3 The sustainability practices of investors

This chapter presents global trends in assets under management by institutional investors taking into account sustainability considerations in their portfolio selection, as well as asset managers' sustainability-related engagement preferences. The chapter also provides an overview of the responses of asset managers investing in Brazil to the OECD survey on sustainability practices.

Investors perspectives

The total assets under management by professional investors that consider environmental, social and governance (ESG) risk factors in portfolio selection and management has grown significantly in the last few years. While the definition of sustainable investment varies between countries and over time, Table 3.1 and Figure 3.1 provide an indicative snapshot of the growing global importance of sustainable investing assets.

Since most of the sustainable investing data rely on survey-based approaches, the large numbers above should be taken with caution because part of the value of sustainable investing assets may be attributed to asset managers who claim to adopt sustainable or ESG-conscious strategies but who do not necessarily contribute to more social and environmental sustainability. This could be either due to misleading investors when labelling a financial product (including the so-called "greenwashing") or because the mandated goals of an investor are not aligned with what the best scientific evidence would recommend. In any circumstance, one fair conclusion can be extracted from the numbers above: asset owners such as pension funds and families have increasingly allocated their portfolios to investment vehicles that purport to be sustainable in Canada, the United States and Japan. In Europe, Australia and New Zealand, it is difficult to draw any conclusion on trends between 2016 and 2020 because of changes in the definition of sustainable investment during that period, but the proportion of sustainable investing assets reported relative to total managed assets was high (above 37%) in Europe, Australia and New Zealand in 2020 (GSI Alliance, 2021[1]).

Table 3.1. Snapshot of global sustainable investing assets

			(USD billions)
	2016	**2018**	**2020**
United States	8 723	11 995	17 081
Europe	12 040	14 075	12 017
Japan	474	2 180	2 874
Canada	1 086	1 699	2 423
Australia and New Zealand	516	734	906
Total	**22 839**	**30 683**	**35 301**

Note: Significant changes in the way sustainable investment is defined have been adopted in Australia, Europe and New Zealand, so direct comparisons across regions and time are not easily made.
Source: GSI Alliance (2021[1]), Global Sustainable Investment Review 2020, http://www.gsi-alliance.org/.

Figure 3.1. Proportion of sustainable investing assets relative to total managed assets

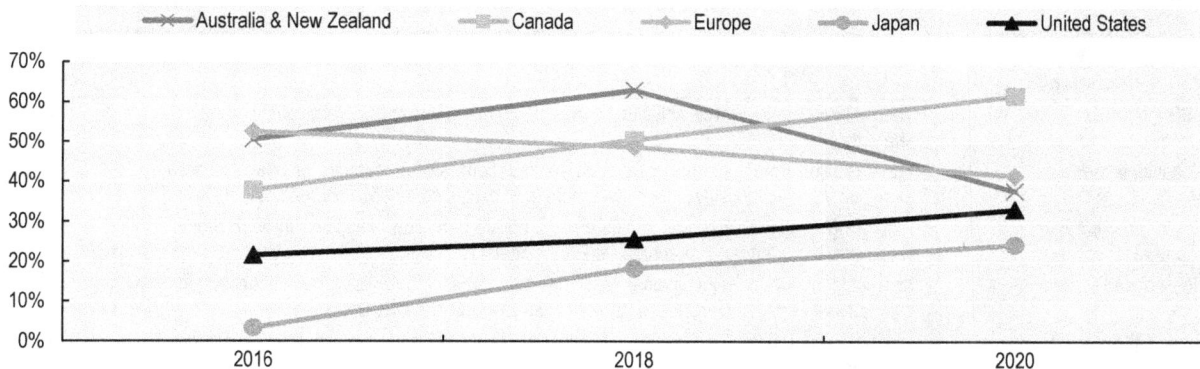

Note: Significant changes in the way sustainable investment is defined have been adopted in Australia, Europe and New Zealand, so direct comparisons between regions and years are not easily made.
Source: GSI Alliance (2021[1]), Global Sustainable Investment Review 2020, http://www.gsi-alliance.org/.

A relatively small subset of the sustainable investing universe is composed of investment funds that label themselves as ESG or sustainable funds – for instance by including "ESG" or "sustainable investing" terms in their names. Focussing only on investment funds and benefiting from a different database than in Table 3.1, it is possible to identify a trend of strong growth in assets under management for these ESG funds[1] that reached USD 1.7 trillion in 2021 (Figure 3.2, Panel A). This was mainly the result of the highest net inflow amounts in 2020 and 2021 with USD 241 billion and USD 586 billion, respectively. While the value of assets under management of climate funds was very modest between 2016 and 2019, during 2020 and 2021 climate funds received comparatively larger amounts of inflows than in previous years with net inflows six and 19 times that of the previous three years' average (2017-19) inflow, respectively. In Brazil, asset under management of ESG funds saw a significant increase in 2021 when the total amount of funds reached to USD 2.4 billion (Figure 3.2, Panel B). Climate funds, however, represent a very small share of total ESG funds in Brazil.

Figure 3.2. Assets under management of funds labelled as or focusing on ESG and climate

A. Global

B. Brazil

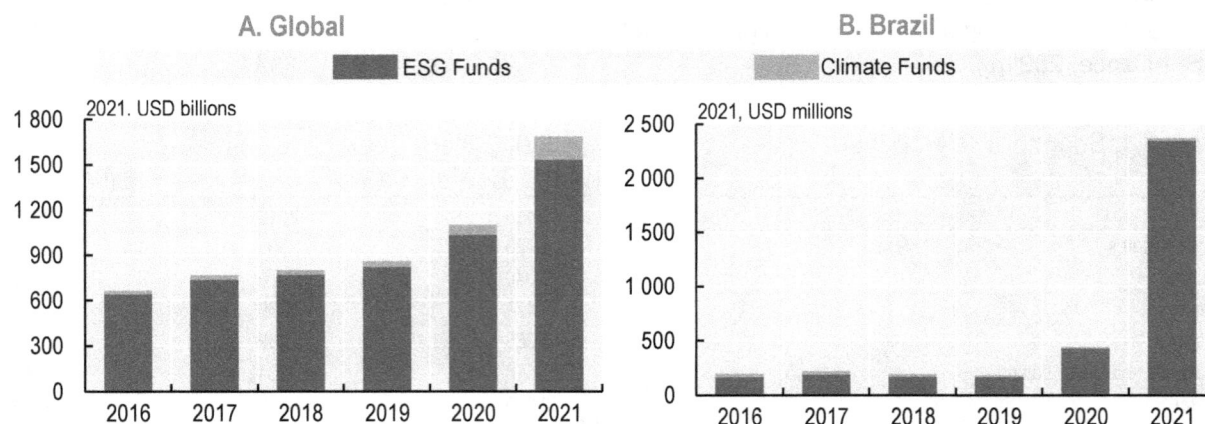

Note: Funds retrieved from Reuters Funds Screen classified as Climate Funds or ESG Funds in the case their names contain, respectively, climate or ESG relevant acronyms and words such as ESG, sustainable, responsible, ethical, green and climate (and their translation in other languages). Funds without any asset value are excluded.
Source: Refinitiv, Datastream, OECD calculations.

Table 3.2. Sustainable investing assets by strategy in 2020

Sustainable investment strategy	Definition	Assets (USD billions)
ESG integration	The systematic and explicit inclusion by investment managers of ESG factors into financial analysis.	25 195
Negative screening	The exclusion from a portfolio of certain sectors, companies, countries or other issuers based on activities considered not investable (e.g. excluding tobacco companies).	15 030
Corporate engagement and shareholder action	Employing shareholder power to influence corporate behaviour, including through proxy voting that is guided by comprehensive ESG guidelines.	10 504
Norm-based screening	Screening of investments against minimum standards of business practice based on international norms such as those issued by the UN, ILO and OECD.	4 140
Sustainability-themed investing	Investing in themes or assets specifically contributing to sustainable solutions (e.g. sustainable agriculture and gender equity).	1 948
Best-in-class screening	Investment in sectors or companies selected for positive ESG performance relative to industry peers, and that achieve a rating above a defined threshold.	1 384
Impact/community investing	Investing to achieve positive social and environmental impact.	352

Note: Asset managers may apply more than one strategy to a given pool of assets, so there is double-counting if one adds all strategies above. For information on the total of sustainable investing assets in 2020, see Table 3.1.
Source: GSI Alliance (2021[1]), Global Sustainable Investment Review 2020, http://www.gsi-alliance.org/.

While the numbers in the table above face the same challenges of categorisation previously mentioned, the following features of the current sustainable investing universe can still be identified:

- the most significant strategy (with USD 25 trillion) focuses on the integration by asset managers of ESG factors into their financial analysis
- strategies that often accept a tangible trade-off between wealth creation and better ESG results ("Impact/community investing") currently add to USD 352 billion[2] (only 1.4% when compared to the "ESG integration" strategy)
- assets under management by investors who claim to employ shareholder power to influence corporate behaviour on ESG-related issues has reached a meaningful value of USD 10.5 trillion.

With respect to environmental factors related to climate change, the value of assets under management in the last item above might even be an underestimation, because some investors who do not have a clear sustainable investing mandate might be nonetheless concerned with their exposure to climate risk and willing to engage with corporates to reduce their risks. For instance, 615 investors (including from Brazil and other emerging markets) with USD 60 trillion in assets under management have so far joined the Climate Action 100+, which is an initiative to ensure the world's largest corporate GHG emitters cut emissions to help achieve the goals of the Paris Agreement (2015[2]). Currently, this initiative focuses on 167 companies representing more than 80% of global industrial emissions, including Petrobras, Suzano and Vale from Brazil.

There is no data for "sustainable investing assets" in Brazil, but a majority of asset managers investing in Brazil – and especially the larger ones – review the sustainability or ESG disclosure of their portfolio companies (see figure below).

Figure 3.3. Asset managers' review of ESG disclosure in Brazil

Question: Do you review the sustainability or ESG disclosures of your portfolio companies?

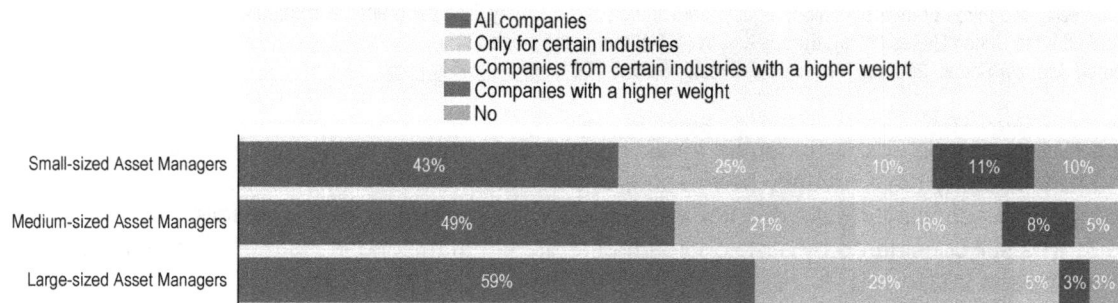

Note: In the survey questionnaire, asset managers could answer or leave this question unanswered. The shares in this table consider only the universe of asset managers that answered the question. On average 92% of the asset managers responded within each size category.
Source: OECD Survey on Sustainability Practices of Asset Managers Investing in Brazil.

Sustainable investing is a wide category that encompasses ESG issues of very different natures, from climate change to human rights. The relative importance of a number of ESG risks from the company perspective is discussed in this report but still from an investor point of view it is possible to see the current preferences of a sample of major global institutional investors in Figure 3.4 (investors not necessarily self-reported as "sustainable investors" with USD 29 trillion in assets under management). In this sample (with some overrepresentation of UK-based investors), it is clear that climate change and associated risks are the number one priority with respect to engagement with companies, followed by human capital management (a social issue), board composition and executive remuneration (governance issues).

Figure 3.4. Global institutional investor engagement preferences in 2020

Question: to what extent do you agree with the following statement? "During the last year, this issue in particular has prompted me to seek engagement with companies"

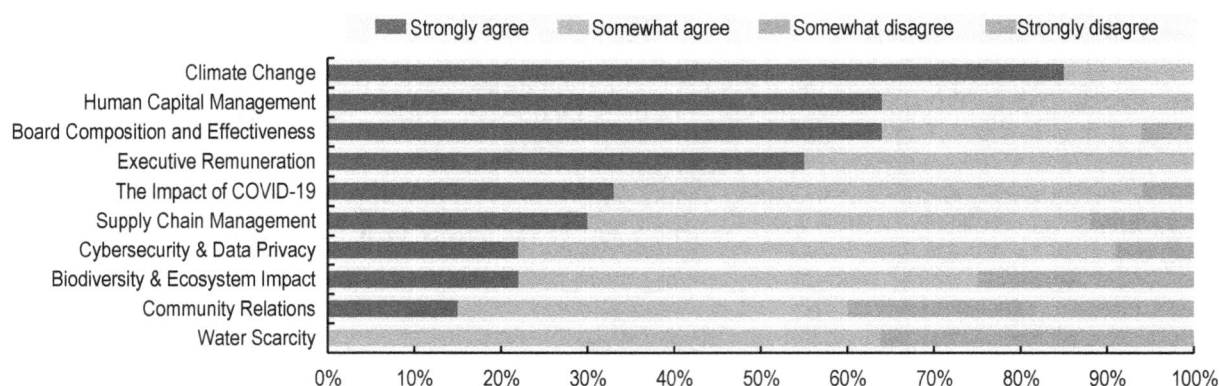

Note: 42 global institutional investors (not necessarily self-reported as "sustainable investors") with USD 29 trillion in assets under management (with nearly two-thirds of their portfolio in equity) participated in the survey. The geographical distribution of those investors was the following: UK (33%); the United States (17%); Europe ex-UK (12%); rest of the world (38%).
Source: Morrow Sodali (2021[3]), Institutional Investor Survey 2021, https://morrowsodali.com/insights/institutional-investor-survey-2021.

Specifically among asset managers investing in Brazil, water and wastewater management, biodiversity and data security have recently been some of their key sustainability priorities (Table 3.3). While climate change and associated risks are not a top priority for surveyed asset managers investing in Brazil, this issue was still considered by a majority of managers when making investment decisions or engaging with companies in 2021.

Table 3.3. The share of issues that were incorporated into an investment decision or prompted asset managers to engage with a company during the last 12 months in Brazil

	A. Large-sized asset managers	B. Medium-sized asset managers	C. Small-sized asset managers
Water & Wastewater Management	85%	68%	61%
Biodiversity and Ecological Impacts	80%	72%	67%
Human Capital	79%	78%	75%
Waste & Hazardous Materials Management	77%	63%	63%
Data Security and Customer Privacy	75%	81%	73%
Human Rights & Community Relations	73%	70%	57%
Supply Chain Management	72%	68%	64%
Climate Change	69%	58%	53%
Air Quality	39%	39%	34%
Other ESG issue	63%	41%	23%

Note: In the survey questionnaire, asset managers could answer "yes", "no" or leave this question unanswered. The shares in this table consider only the universe of companies that answered either "yes" or "no", which is slightly different for each one of the sustainability issues. For instance, 335 asset managers provided an answer related to "Climate Change", while only 319 answered with respect to the topic "Air Quality". Overall, on average more than 90% of the asset managers responded with respected to all of the sustainability issues.
Source: OECD Survey on Sustainability Practices of Asset Managers Investing in Brazil.

References

GIIN (2020), *Annual Impact Investor Survey 2020*, https://thegiin.org/research/publication/impinv-survey-2020. [4]

GSI Alliance, G. (2021), *Global Sustainable Investment Review 2020*, http://www.gsi-alliance.org/. [1]

Morrow Sodali (2021), *Institutional Investor Survey 2021*, https://morrowsodali.com/insights/institutional-investor-survey-2021. [3]

UNFCCC (2015), *The Paris Agreement*, https://unfccc.int/sites/default/files/english_paris_agreement.pdf. [2]

Notes

[1] Funds retrieved from the Reuters Funds Screen were classified as Climate Funds or ESG Funds in the case their names contain, respectively, climate or ESG relevant acronyms and words such as ESG, sustainable, responsible, ethical, green and climate (and their translation in other languages).

[2] According to another estimate, the impact investing market size worldwide (including Brazil and other emerging markets) would be equal to USD 715 billion as of the end of 2019 (GIIN, 2020[4]).

4 Company sustainability standards and frameworks

The chapter summarises the most commonly used sustainability reporting standards and presents their use by listed companies globally. It also covers use and preferences of reporting standards by public companies in Brazil. The chapter then summarises the main concepts of materiality for corporate disclosure and discusses the main challenges related to the adoption of each concept. It also analyses the market value of companies in industries where sustainability issues is considered to be financially material in Brazil and in selected countries. The chapter concludes with an overview of the current regulatory framework for sustainability disclosure in Brazil.

Nowadays, companies use a great number of frameworks and standards to disclose information on their climate-related and other ESG performance, risks and strategy. Table 4.1 summarises the most often used frameworks and standards[1] with respect to how detailed they are, their targeted audience, issues they cover and the threshold they recommend for information to be disclosed (i.e. which issues would be material for the framework). Possible definitions of "materiality" are discussed in more detail further below, but, concisely, corporate disclosure is "financially material" if it could reasonably be expected to influence an investor or a lender's analysis of a company's future cash flows. A "double materiality" concept incorporates what is financially material, but it also includes within its scope information that would be relevant to multiple stakeholders' understanding of a company's effect on the environment, on people or on society (e.g. for consumers and employees).

Table 4.1. Climate-related and other ESG reporting frameworks and standards

Institution	System	Level of detail	Materiality	Audience	Issues
FSB's TCFD	TCFD recommendations	Principles-based[1]	Financially material	Investors, lenders and insurance underwriters	Climate-related issues
IFRS Foundation – International Sustainability Standards Board (ISSB)[2]	IFRS Sustainability Standards[2]	Detailed information	Financially material	Investors	Initial focus on climate-related issues, but with a plan to cover a great number of ESG issues
Value Reporting Foundation – SASB Standards Board[3]	SASB Standards	Detailed information	Financially material	Investors	A great number of ESG issues, with subset of standards in each of 77 industries
Value Reporting Foundation – Integrated Reporting Framework Board[3]	<IR> Framework	Principles-based	Financially material	Investors	A great number of ESG issues
Global Sustainability Standards Board (GSSB)	GRI Standards	Detailed information	Double materiality	Multiple stakeholders	A great number of ESG issues, with a plan to have a subset of standards in each of 40 sectors
GHG Protocol	GHG Protocol Corporate Standards	Detailed information	-[4]	-[4]	GHG emissions[4]
CDP (previously "Carbon Disclosure Project")	CDP questionnaires[5]	Detailed information	-[5]	Investors and customers	Climate change, forests and water security[5]
Climate Disclosure Standards Board (CDSB)[6]	CDSB Framework	Principles-based	Financially material and relevant[7]	Investors	Climate and other environmental information

Notes:

1: While TCFD's recommendations (TCFD, 2017[1]) are indeed principles-based, the Task Force has published a number of documents providing detailed guidance on how to better comply with its recommendations, such as the report "Guidance on Scenario Analysis for Non-Financial Companies" (TCFD, 2020[2]). To some extent, therefore, this set of recommendations and guidance documents on how companies may disclose financially material information, preferably in mainstream financial filings, would together demand "detailed information" according to the classification in the third column of this table.

2: IFRS Foundation announced in November 2021 the formation of the International Sustainability Standards Board ("ISSB"), which will sit alongside the International Accounting Standards Board ("IASB"), to set IFRS Sustainability Disclosure Standards. In the same opportunity, IFRS Foundation committed to consolidate with the Value Reporting Foundation Board and CDSB by June 2022. IFRS Foundation's recently amended constitution provides that IFRS Sustainability Disclosure Standards "are intended to result in the provision of high-quality, transparent and comparable information [...] in sustainability disclosures that is useful to investors and other participants in the world's capital markets in making economic decisions" (item 2.a).

3: SASB Standards Board and Integrated Reporting Framework Board ("<IR> Framework Board") merged in June 2021. Currently, both standard-setting boards are supervised by a newly created organisation called Value Reporting Foundation Board ("VRF"). In November 2021, the VRF committed to consolidate into the IFRS Foundation by June 2022.

4: GHG Protocol's corporate accounting and reporting standard provides requirements and guidance for companies preparing a corporate-level GHG emissions inventory. It does not adopt a materiality concept, and other ESG reporting frameworks and standards will typically either require or allow GHG emissions to be disclosed according to GHG Protocol's standard. In this standard, GHG emissions are classified under three categories: Scope 1 (direct emissions from a company's own operations); Scope 2 (emissions from purchased or acquired electricity, steam, heat and cooling); Scope 3 (the entire chain emissions impact from the goods the company purchases to the products it sells).

5: CDP's questionnaires would not be considered a reporting framework or standard in the traditional sense, but the institution offers a widely used system for companies to answer to any of the following questionnaires: Climate Change; Forests; Water Security. The questionnaires are meant to be disclosed to (i) investors or to (ii) customers interested in assessing the environmental impact of their supply chain. Corporate management is not supposed to make a materiality assessment of the information to disclose, because CDP offers a set of questions by economic sector and companies have strong incentives to answer all of them in order to receive better scorings calculated by CDP's system. Questionnaires are shortened only for companies with an annual revenue of less than EUR/USD 250 million and corporates answering the questionnaire for the first time.

6: In January 2022, the CDSB consolidated into the IFRS Foundation.

7: According to the CDSB Framework, environmental information should be disclosed if financially material or relevant. "Relevant" in this context would be information that might be financially material at some point, while the link between the information and future cash flows is not evident. In either case, GHG emissions shall be reported in all cases regardless of management's assessment of their materiality or relevance (CDSB, 2019[3]).

Source: Standards, frameworks and websites of the institutions visited in July and November 2021 and January 2022; OECD elaboration.

For a company that is choosing which reporting framework to use or for a regulator that is considering whether to recommend or require a particular framework, a first question could be which broad issues are the most relevant to the company and to the market (last column in Table 4.1). For instance, TCFD recommendations cover climate-related risks only, while the SASB Board and GSSB offer reporting standards on a full breadth of ESG issues. Therefore, for example, if climate-related risks are the most material risks in a specific context, compliance with the TCFD recommendations might be more relevant to advance on as an initial focus, before considering whether to report on other environmental and social dimensions, using SASB or GRI reporting standards for instance.

Another question for companies and regulators assessing existing ESG reporting frameworks is who would be the primary users of the information to be disclosed (the fifth column in Table 4.1). A large majority of existing ESG reporting frameworks cite investors in equity and debt as their main audience with the notable exceptions of the GRI Standards, which aim at being used by shareholders and multiple stakeholders, and CDP's questionnaires, which have both investors and supply chain customers as their audience. A focus on the information needs of existing and potential investors and lenders has been traditionally adopted by financial reporting standards (IASB, 2018[4]). However, as important as the definition of the main audience of the disclosure may be, the disclosed information might still be relevant to users that are not considered primary. For instance, CO_2 emissions will likely be relevant to shareholders of an oil and gas company as primary users due to the potential cash flow impact of carbon pricing policies in the future, but it may also be of interest to consumers or environmentally conscious employees who would prefer to work in a low-carbon company.

The definition of materiality in an ESG disclosure framework or standard goes largely hand in hand with the portrait of its primary users (fourth column in Table 4.1). If the primary users are investors, it is often assumed that they make investment and voting decisions mostly based on a company's expected future cash flows and their timing. Only the CDSB Framework – which focuses only on environmental and climate change information and considers investors the primary users – somewhat diverges from this general rule in two ways: (i) requiring disclosure of information even if its impact on a company's cash flows is not evident but could become relevant; (ii) mandating transparency of GHG emissions in all cases regardless of management's assessment of its materiality.

ESG reporting frameworks and standards summarised in Table 4.1 also vary with respect to the level of detail of their guidance and requirements (see third column). Some of them are principles-based, which allows for flexibility when implemented by companies with different characteristics and operating in different countries. Flexibility, however, makes consistency across time and comparability between companies more difficult, and that is why some ESG reporting standards provide greater detail on how companies should account and report on sustainability information.

In either case, two additional features of ESG reporting should be highlighted. First, companies may choose to report sustainability information based on two different standards with similar issues' coverage, as long as they clearly segment the disclosed information (for instance, according to SASB for investors and GRI standards for a wider public). Second, a principles-based framework may serve as the overall guidance to management when reporting sustainability information according to a more detailed standard (for instance, using the <IR> Framework when developing a sustainability report with information required by SASB Standards).

TCFD recommendations receive particular attention in this report because, in September 2021, the Central Bank of Brazil (BCB) announced mandatory disclosure aligned with the TCFD's recommendation for financial institutions (BCB, 2021[5]). In a first phase, the rule will require the disclosure of qualitative aspects related to governance, strategy and risk management, and, in a second phase, quantitative information will also be required. The Task Force's recommendations suggest the disclosure of financially material information, preferably in mainstream financial filings, around four thematic areas (TCFD, 2017[1]):

a. Governance – the organisation's governance around climate-related risks and opportunities

b. Strategy – the impacts of climate-related matters on the organisation's strategy.

c. Risk management – the processes used by the organisation to identify, assess and manage climate-related risks

d. Metrics and targets – the metrics and targets used to assess and manage relevant climate-related risks and opportunities, including greenhouse gas emissions.

This plenitude of existing standards and frameworks (seven in Table 4.1) raises the question of whether climate-related information is comparable between companies that effectively disclose them. Figure 4.1 presents the use of the abovementioned ESG standards and frameworks by Brazilian companies in 2021.

Figure 4.1. Use of ESG reporting standards by Brazilian public companies in 2021

A. Responses from IBOVESPA companies

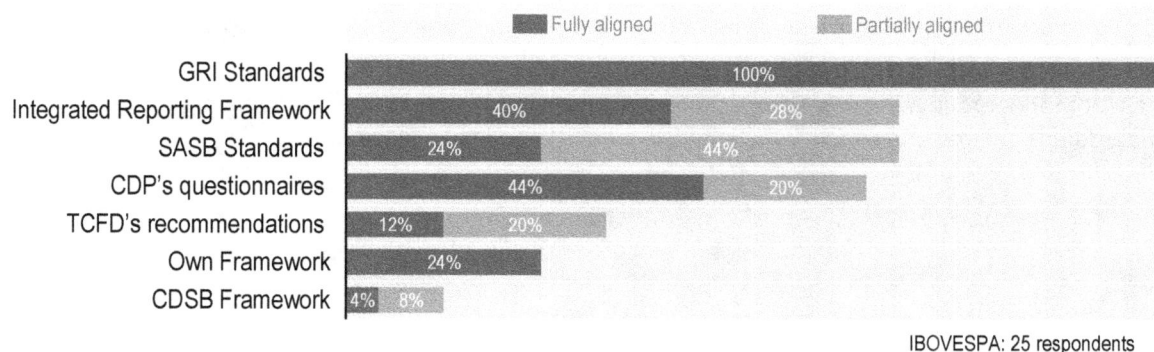

B. Responses of other companies

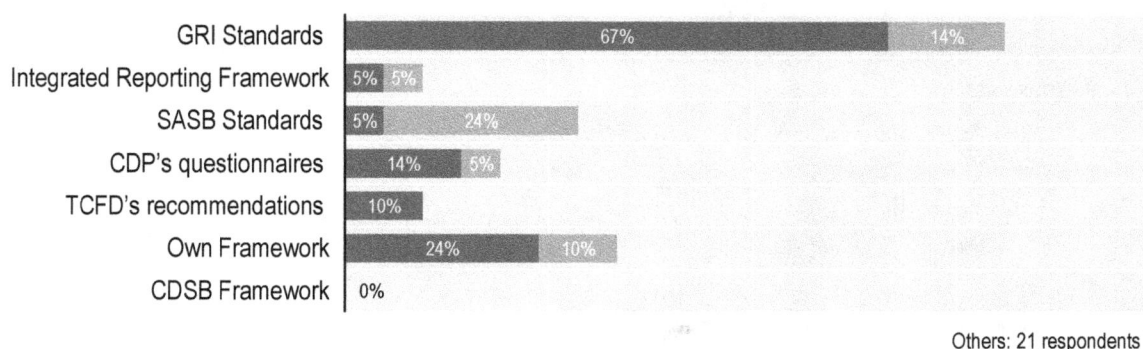

Note: Some sustainability reports followed more than one ESG reporting standard, and this is the reason why the percentages in each graph do not add up to 100%.
Source: OECD Survey on Sustainability Practices of Public Companies in Brazil.

While overlaps and conflicting requirements between ESG reporting standards and frameworks are not assessed in this report, Figure 4.2 shows that global investors do have clear preferences for some ESG standards, which may suggest that existing standards are indeed significantly different.

Figure 4.2. Global institutional investors ESG reporting preferences in 2020

Question: What is your preferred ESG framework for companies to best disclose their material ESG topics?

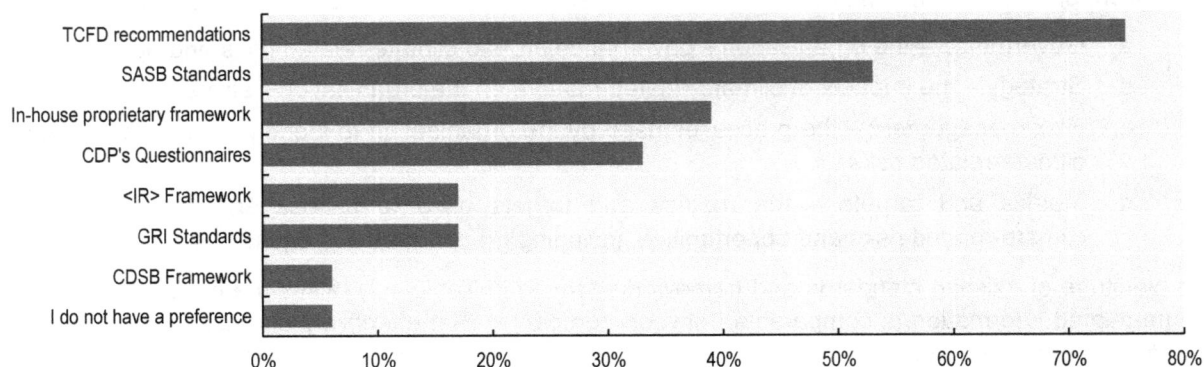

Notes:
1: For information on respondents to the survey, see notes to Figure 3.4.
2: Respondents to the survey could choose more than one preferred ESG framework, what explains why the numbers in this figure add to more than 100%. Specifically, the survey found that a number of institutional investors, including BlackRock, State Street Global Advisors and Vanguard, have called out TCFD recommendations and SASB Standards as the two ESG frameworks that listed companies should follow.
Source: Morrow Sodali (2021, p. 17[6]), Institutional Investor Survey 2021, https://morrowsodali.com/insights/institutional-investor-survey-2021.

For asset managers investing in Brazil, preferences are less clear with a relatively higher priority for GRI Standards and a smaller one for TCFD's recommendations (see Figure 4.3).

Figure 4.3. Preference of ESG reporting standards by asset managers investing in Brazil in 2021

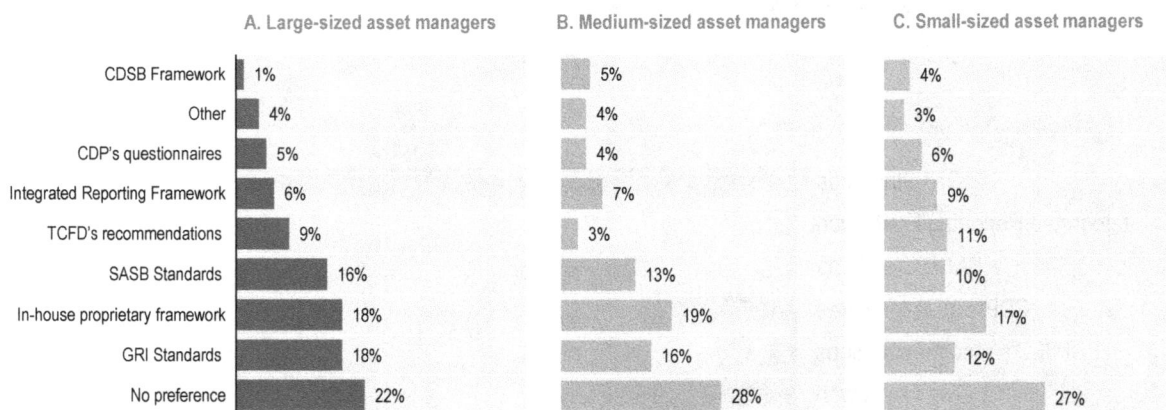

Note: In the survey questionnaire, asset managers selected their preferred ESG reporting standard. The shares in this table consider only the universe of asset managers that provided their preferences. Importantly, it was possible for any asset manager to indicate more than a standard as their preferred one.
Source: OECD Survey on Sustainability Practices of Asset Managers Investing in Brazil.

Materiality

An essential part of any reporting system is the criteria to choose which pieces of information must be communicated to end-users. In the case of companies, the term often used to refer to this assessment is "materiality": whether a piece of information is material enough for its primary users to justify the costs of collecting the information and disclosing it. Clearly, a case-by-case costs and benefits analysis of the materiality of every piece of information would not be feasible, so the implementation of the materiality concept depends to a large extent on reporting standards, securities regulators' guidance and practices widely accepted in the capital markets.

Information has traditionally been considered material if it could reasonably be expected to influence an investor's or a creditor's analysis of a company's future cash flows. For instance, the International Accounting Standards Board (IASB) provides that "information is material if omitting, misstating or obscuring it could reasonably be expected to influence the decisions that the primary users of general purpose financial reports make on the basis of those reports, which provide financial information about a specific reporting entity" (2018, p. A22[4]). In an often-cited precedent, the US Supreme Court clarified that "an omitted fact is material if there is a substantial likelihood that a reasonable shareholder would consider it important in deciding how to vote. [...] Put another way, there must be a substantial likelihood that the disclosure of the omitted fact would have been viewed by the reasonable investor as having significantly altered the 'total mix' of information made available" (*TSC Industries, Inc.* v. *Northway, Inc.*). The aforementioned materiality concept can be labelled "financial materiality", and, as detailed in Table 4.1, not only financial reporting standards but also a number of ESG reporting frameworks and standards adopt a "financial materiality" approach.

More recently, a "double materiality" concept has been adopted in some sustainability reporting frameworks, defining as material information that – in addition to being financially relevant to investors – would be pertinent to multiple stakeholders' understanding of a company's effect on the environment and on people (e.g. for consumers, employees and communities). For example, the 2014 EU Non-Financial Reporting Directive provides that a company subject to the directive is required to disclose information "to the extent necessary for an understanding of the undertaking's development, performance, position and impact of its activity, relating to, as a minimum, environmental, social and employee matters, respect for human rights, anti-corruption and bribery matters" (Article 19a, item 1).

While in theory clearly distinct, the frontiers between financial and double materiality may be rather fluid in practice. For instance, in what constitutes one aspect of "dynamic materiality" (WEF, 2020, p. 8[7]), a risk that does not seem to be financially material in a moment in time (e.g. GHG emissions in a country with a poor environmental track-record) may gradually or quickly become financially relevant if the social context changes (in the same example, if a climate-conscious political leadership comes to power). In some contexts, economically irrelevant ESG risks that are material for a society may be expected at some point to become financially material for a company, either through society's pressure for a switch in public policy (e.g. regulation that makes companies internalise externalities) or consumers' and employees' change of preferences (making companies voluntarily change their businesses). To some extent, therefore, the time-horizon used in the materiality analysis seems to be also key: the longer the time-horizon, the larger the potential for overlap between financial and double materiality (IOSCO, 2021, pp. 28-30[8]).

Regardless of the time horizon, it should also be noted that even in the shorter term there might also be a significant overlap between information items that are material both to a company's cash flows and to society as a whole. To take the example of a company in the mining sector, Vale disclosed in 2021 its Scope 1 GHG emissions as required both by SASB and GRI standards (respectively, as seen in Table 4.1, they follow a financial and double materiality concepts). The same company also disclosed, among climate-related items, Scopes 2 and 3 GHG emissions and the energy intensity of its operations, but, in those cases, only to align itself with the GRI Standards (Vale, 2021, pp. 108-111; 174[9]).

By definition, "double materiality" requires wider disclosure than "financial materiality" because the former includes the latter (the example in the paragraph above concretely shows it). Since collecting information and disclosing it present a relatively fixed cost for a company (somewhat independent from its size), a mandatory requirement to disclose ESG information according to a double materiality standard would represent a greater relative cost for SMEs when compared to larger companies (OECD, 2022, p. 34[10]). Moreover, if disclosure is only mandatory for listed companies, it might represent a disincentive for companies to go public.

Another challenge for policy makers considering to mandate an ESG disclosure regime based on "double materiality" rather than "financial materiality" would be the transition and longer-term costs it would create for some key capital markets actors other than companies, namely for securities regulators and auditors. First, there would be a short-term cost for changing systems and rules that were typically based on the assumption that corporate information to be disclosed should be material for investors. For instance, securities regulators that have a legal mandate only to protect investors and to maintain fair, efficient and transparent markets might need to have their powers enlarged to also include addressing systemic risks or non-financially material ESG risks more broadly. In the case of Brazil, CMV has a broad mandate, including, for instance, the goals of promoting the efficiency of capital markets and of ensuring public access to listed companies' information (art. 4 of Law 6 385 from 1976). This mandate would arguably allow Brazil's securities regulator to require sustainability disclosure based on "double materiality", but there would still be a risk of litigation involving the regulator's legal mandate since this regulatory option has not yet been examined by the courts.

Second, if key capital market actors become responsible for analysing information beyond their core expertise in corporate finance, they might become less efficient as a result. For example, securities regulators would need to supervise risks that have been (and will probably continue to be) overseen by environmental agencies, potentially duplicating work and offering conflicting guidance on non-financial materiality in some circumstances. Likewise, the assessment of what is material for the society as a whole requires the use of techniques, reference points and data from the public policy discipline, which are not often mastered by corporate finance experts and may be expensive (e.g. surveys to assess the preferences of a great number of individuals).

Much of the relevance of the discussion above would dissipate if investors were as concerned with their investees' impact on society as they are with their long-term financial results. If this were the case, a company's impact on society and the environment would necessarily become financially material because investors would be willing to accept smaller returns in exchange for positive contributions for society (i.e. a company's cost of capital would be smaller).

The evidence so far is that global investors continue to be by and large more concerned with the financial performance of their assets (as seen in Table 3.2, strategies that often accept a tangible trade-off between wealth creation and better ESG results do not currently represent a significant share of assets under management) and major global investors are especially interested in sustainability information that is financially material (as shown in Figure 4.2, TCFD recommendations and SASB Standards – which follow a financial materiality criterion – are by far the preferred ESG framework by institutional investors).

The evidence for asset managers investing in Brazil, however, is less clear-cut. As presented in Figure 4.3, they have a slightly higher preference for the GRI Standards, which follow a double materiality criterion. Likewise, as shown in Figure 4.4 below, a majority of asset managers investing in Brazil said they would be willing to accept a lower rate of return in exchange for societal or environmental benefits (it should be noted, nonetheless, that the question did not estipulate by how much lower).

Figure 4.4. Asset managers investing in Brazil: willingness to trade-off financial returns

Question: Would you be willing to accept a lower rate of return as an investor in a company in exchange for societal or environmental benefits?

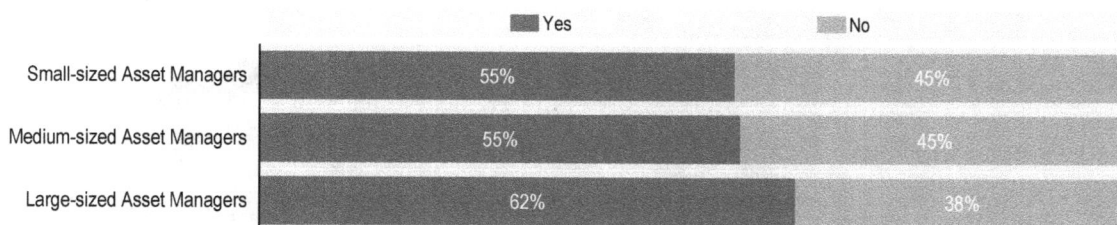

Note: In the survey questionnaire, asset managers could answer "yes", "no" or leave this question unanswered. The shares in this table consider only the universe of asset managers that answered either "yes" or "no". On average 76% of the asset managers responded within each size category.
Source: OECD Survey on Sustainability Practices of Asset Managers Investing in Brazil.

ESG accounting and reporting frameworks

Brazil and many other jurisdictions do not currently mandate the use of a specific ESG reporting framework or standard (in the case of Brazil, with the exception of financial institutions as mentioned in Chapter 3). This freedom has led corporations to adopt a number of different standards or, in some cases, disclose only some information items foreseen in a specific standard (see often used standards by Brazilian public companies in (Figure 4.1).

The lack of comparability between companies' sustainability information harms investors' capacity to adequately value each company and, therefore, to decide how to allocate their capital and engage with companies. In other words, capital markets are less efficient if companies do not disclose sustainability information that is financially material or if their disclosures are difficult to compare. Likewise, disclosure of material risks is essential for investors to effectively manage the aggregate risks of their portfolios, and for financial stability supervisors to anticipate systemic risks.

The importance of comparability was underlined in a survey recently conducted by International Organization of Securities Commissions ("IOSCO") of 60 asset managers across 19 jurisdictions on sustainability information for investment decisions. The survey identified the creation and adoption of a mandatory common international standard reporting as the most important area for improvement with respect to sustainability (IOSCO, 2021, p. 18[8]). Similarly, a 2019 survey with investors representing 27 asset managers and 30 asset owners from Asia, Europe and the United States found that 75% of them agreed with the statement that "there should be one sustainability-reporting standard" and 82% concurred that "companies should be required by law to issue sustainability reports" (McKinsey & Co., 2019, p. 3[11]).

As presented in the figure below, a similar strong support to require Brazilian public companies to issue sustainability reports is also found among asset managers investing in the country.

Figure 4.5. Asset managers' support for mandatory corporate sustainability disclosure in Brazil

Question: Would you support a mandatory regulation requiring all Brazilian listed companies to disclose an annual sustainability report with ESG information that is financially material for them?

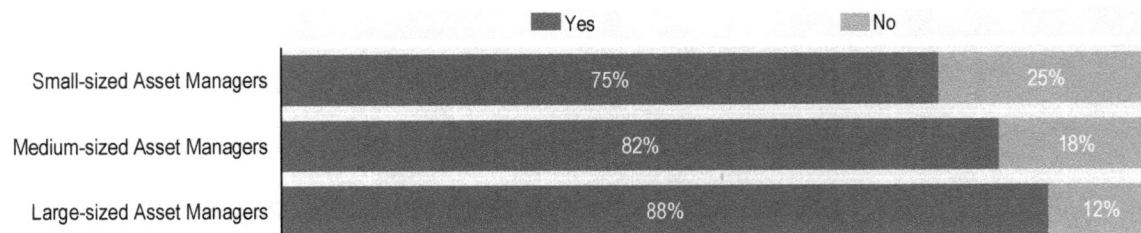

Note: In the survey questionnaire, asset managers could answer "yes", "no" or leave this question unanswered. The shares in this table consider only the universe of asset managers that answered either "yes" or "no". On average 93% of the asset managers responded within each size category.
Source: OECD Survey on Sustainability Practices of Asset Managers Investing in Brazil.

In a very concrete way, the adoption of multiple ESG reporting standards also creates costs for corporations, which may have to either comply with different reporting standards or respond to ad hoc information requests by institutional investors interested in comparing results and business prospects of their investees. Moreover, directors and key executives may be interested in benchmarking their non-financial performance against their peers in order to better identify where improvement is needed or claim their success if their results are above-average. This may explain why, in the same aforementioned 2019 survey, 58% of executives representing 50 companies from Asia, Europe and the United States agreed with the statement that "there should be one sustainability-reporting standard" and 66% concurred that "companies should be required by law to issue sustainability reports" (McKinsey & Co., 2019, p. 3[11]). In Brazil, the support among public companies for mandatory sustainability disclosure is even higher (see figure below).

Figure 4.6. Public companies' support for mandatory corporate sustainability disclosure in Brazil

Question: Would you support a regulation obliging all Brazilian listed companies to disclose an annual sustainability report with ESG information that is financially material for them?

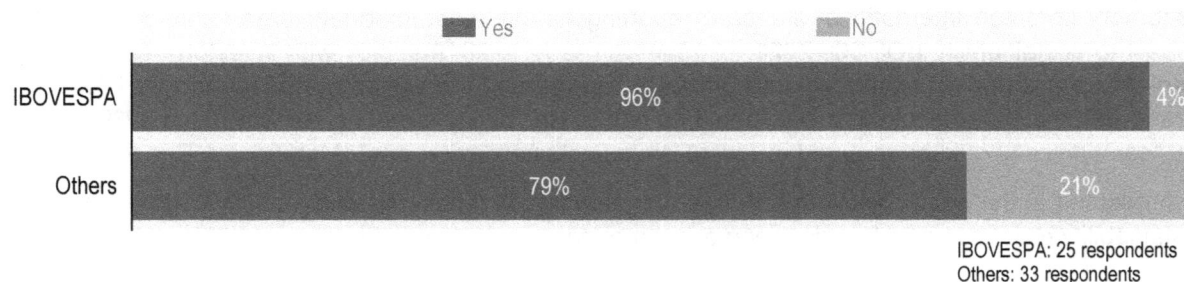

IBOVESPA: 25 respondents
Others: 33 respondents

Source: OECD Survey on Sustainability Practices of Public Companies in Brazil.

Some jurisdictions have already established regulations or initiated public consultations or legislative proposals to mandate companies to disclose sustainability information according to a specific reporting standard. There are two main challenges in such processes: (i) the definition of the group of companies that will be subject to the new disclosure obligation; (ii) the co-ordination across jurisdictions to adopt – if not the same reporting standard – at least to develop some core guidance and metrics that could be identical in all markets.

As discussed above, disclosure requirements often represent a greater relative cost for SMEs when compared to larger companies and, if disclosure is only mandatory for listed companies, sustainability disclosure requirements might represent a disincentive for some companies to go public. With respect to disclosure costs, it should be noted that there are not only direct costs such as developing internal control systems and hiring an external auditor, but there are also indirect costs such as revealing information that may be useful for competitors. Having those challenges in mind, policy makers have devised financial information rules that are flexible according to the size of the company or its stage of development, for instance providing a waiver from some non-essential disclosure requirements for emerging growth companies (OECD, 2018, pp. 17-18[12]).

In considering a path towards greater comparability, the experience of adopting IFRS Standards across most jurisdictions on a global basis can serve as a reference. In total, 144 jurisdictions required the use of IFRS Standards for all or most domestic listed companies as of 2018 (IFRS Foundation, 2018[13]). This successful experience is probably the reason why the IFRS Foundation November 2021 announcement that it would amend its constitution to accommodate an International Sustainability Standards Board ("ISSB") within its structure has been met with enthusiasm by a number of jurisdictions and the IOSCO (see more below).

The ISSB will build on the work of existing investor-focused sustainability reporting initiatives to set IFRS Sustainability Disclosure Standards. The IFRS Foundation's recently amended constitution provides that IFRS Sustainability Disclosure Standards "are intended to result in the provision of high-quality, transparent and comparable information […] in sustainability disclosures that is useful to investors and other participants in the world's capital markets in making economic decisions" (item 2.a). Likewise, by June 2022 this new board will merge with the CDSB, SASB Standards Board and <IR> Framework Board to consolidate their technical expertise, content, staff and other resources (for more information on those boards, see Table 4.1). In this context, the Technical Readiness Working Group (TRWG) – a group formed by the IFRS Foundation Trustees to undertake preparatory work for the ISSB[2] – has already published a prototype climate standard building on the TCFD's recommendations and another prototype document on general disclosure requirements for consideration by the ISSB in its initial work plan (IFRS Foundation, 2021[14]).

Of special interest is the IFRS Foundation's views of a "building blocks" approach and an initial priority for climate-related matters in the work of the planned ISSB (IFRS Foundation, 2021, p. 5[15]). This would mean that ISSB would co-operate with standard-setters from key jurisdictions in order to have a globally consistent set of core standards that would allow the comparability of sustainability reports in those jurisdictions, and expect that standard-setters from smaller markets would eventually adhere to this global reporting baseline. The "building blocks" strategy may also allow, for instance, globally accepted standards based on a financial materiality criterion but with the flexibility for complementary regional or national standards requiring disclosure on matters deemed material only from a "double materiality" perspective.

The IFRS Foundation's decision to initially focus on climate-related matters before working towards other ESG issues is also interesting from a practical point of view. Local standard-setters may be willing to wait for the establishment of global sustainability standards by the ISSB – instead of creating their own – if they foresee in the short term a standard on one of the most pressing ESG issues. Indeed, as shown in Figure 4.10, despite some regional variations, climate-related risks are financially material for an important share of companies by market value globally (more than other environmental risks), representing 65% of the total market capitalisation.

As presented in Figure 4.7 and Figure 4.8, a majority of both Brazilian public companies and asset managers investing in the country support the adoption of an international standard for companies listed in Brazil that either voluntarily or compulsorily disclose an annual sustainability report.

Figure 4.7. Asset managers' support for the adoption of an ESG reporting standard in Brazil

Question: Would you support the adoption of an ESG reporting standard for Brazilian listed companies that either voluntarily or compulsorily disclose an annual sustainability report?

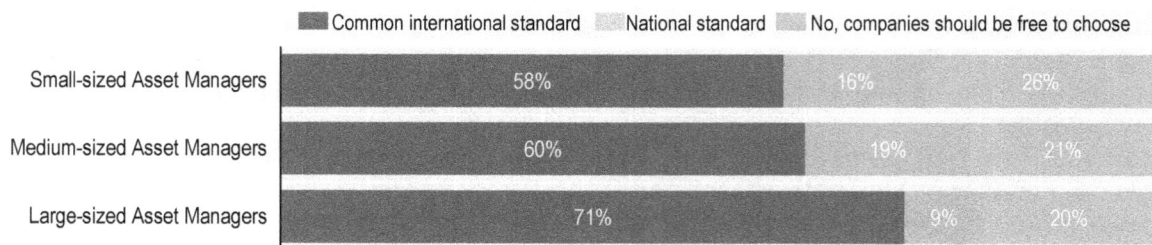

■ Common international standard ▨ National standard ▨ No, companies should be free to choose

Small-sized Asset Managers	58%	16%	26%
Medium-sized Asset Managers	60%	19%	21%
Large-sized Asset Managers	71%	9%	20%

Note: In the survey questionnaire, asset managers could leave this question unanswered. The shares in this table consider only the universe of asset managers that chose one of the available alternatives. On average 90% of the asset managers responded within each size category.
Source: OECD Survey on Sustainability Practices of Asset Managers Investing in Brazil.

Figure 4.8. Public companies' support for the adoption of an ESG reporting standard in Brazil

Question: Would you support the adoption of an ESG reporting standard for Brazilian listed companies that either voluntarily or compulsorily disclose an annual sustainability report?

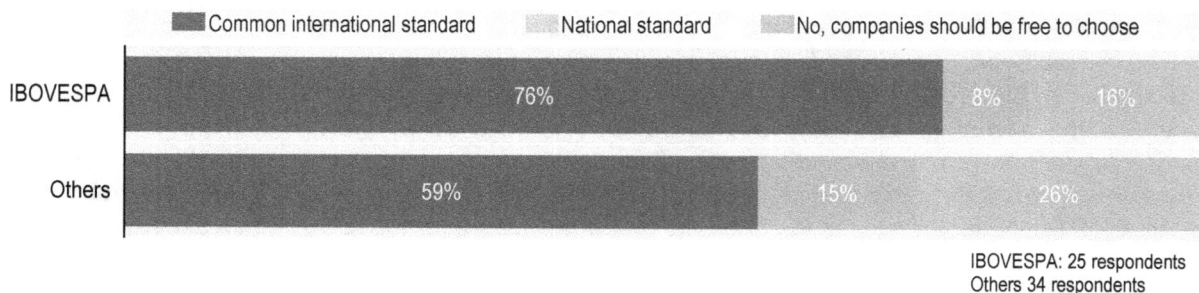

■ Common international standard ▨ National standard ▨ No, companies should be free to choose

IBOVESPA	76%	8%	16%
Others	59%	15%	26%

IBOVESPA: 25 respondents
Others 34 respondents

Source: OECD Survey on Sustainability Practices of Public Companies in Brazil.

Most relevant sustainability risks in Brazil

There are many sustainability issues a company can cover in its sustainability report. For instance, the SASB Sustainable Industry Classification System® Taxonomy ("SASB mapping"),[3] which is set by the SASB Board,[4] presents 26 sustainability issues categorised into five dimensions (see them all in Table 4.4 below). While challenging to decide which issues are financially material for an individual company, it may often be a feasible task. SASB mapping itself offers a classification of which issues would be financially material in each of 77 industries in total. Directors and shareholders may also engage and eventually agree on the most relevant sustainability issues for their company.

A securities regulator that is considering to require sustainability disclosure from public companies, however, may be in a more difficult position. Mandating the disclosure of information related to only some sustainability issues in an initial phase may be the best option because the regulator and market participants may then focus their scarce resources in understanding a manageable number of issues. Ideally, the issues prioritised by the regulator would be those that are overall more relevant to investors and companies in the specific market. There are at least the following four ways to make this assessment:

a. to ask investors which sustainability issues they have recently incorporated into an investment decision or prompted them to engage with a company.

b. to observe which sustainability issues have been included in shareholder resolutions, which is one of the forms of engagement between shareholders and companies.

c. to survey companies on which sustainability issues have been considered by their boards.

d. to use the market capitalisation in each industry in order to calculate the relative importance of all sustainability issues in SASB mapping.

As seen in Table 3.3, water and wastewater management, biodiversity, human capital and data security have recently been some of asset managers investing in Brazil sustainability priorities. While climate change and associated risks are not a top priority for surveyed asset managers investing in Brazil, this issue was still considered by a majority of managers when making investment decisions or engaging with companies in 2021.

As shown in Table 4.2 below, human capital, climate change, biodiversity and data security have been the most frequent sustainability issues in shareholder resolutions from 2019 to 2021 in Brazil. This is broadly in line with asset managers overall preferences when making investment decision and engaging.

Table 4.2. ESG-related shareholder resolution voted in a shareholders` meeting in the last 36 months, by sustainability issue

	IBOVESPA	Others	All
Human Capital	2	4	6
Climate Change	2	3	5
Biodiversity and Ecological Impacts	-	5	5
Data Security and Customer Privacy	-	4	4
Water & Wastewater Management	-	3	3
Supply Chain Management	-	3	3
Waste & Hazardous Materials Management	-	2	2
Human Rights & Community Relations	-	2	2
Air Quality	-	1	1
Other ESG issue	4	-	4
No ESG-related Resolution	15	18	33

Notes:
1: In the survey questionnaire, companies could answer "yes", "no" or leave this question unanswered. If a company had more than one shareholder resolution on the same ESG issue during the 36-month period, it counts only as one in this table. Nevertheless, there are companies with more than one ESG-related shareholder resolution on different sustainability issues during the last 36 months and, in these cases, each different shareholder resolution is counted in the relevant line.
2: The survey questionnaire only presented the nine sustainability issues listed in this table, which often have the exact same names as these issues are presented in the SASB mapping (respondents could also add "other ESG issues"). In order to facilitate answers and to make the results more easily comparable with other similar surveys, the OECD questionnaire merged some sustainability issues in the SASB mapping: "Climate Change" (SASB mapping has three climate-related issues); "Human Capital" (three SASB mapping issues); "Data Security and Customer Privacy" (two SASB mapping issues).
Source: OECD Survey on Sustainability Practices of Public Companies in Brazil.

From the perspective of directors in Brazilian public companies, there is a clear priority for considerations and information involving human capital and data security. In 2021, about 90% of surveyed companies' boards considered these two sustainability issues in their decision-making process (Table 4.3). Among other issues, climate change and biodiversity have also received attention from a majority of public companies' boards in 2021.

Table 4.3. Share of companies whose board of directors considered sustainability issues during the last 12 months

	IBOVESPA	Others
Human Capital	92%	90%
Data Security and Customer Privacy	92%	88%
Human Rights & Community Relations	71%	67%
Climate Change	70%	55%
Supply Chain Management	61%	66%
Biodiversity and Ecological Impacts	52%	58%
Water & Wastewater Management	43%	59%
Waste & Hazardous Materials Management	43%	58%
Air Quality	19%	26%
Other ESG issue	77%	52%

Notes:

1: In the survey questionnaire, companies could answer "yes", "no" or leave this question unanswered. The shares in this table consider only the universe of companies that answered either "yes" or "no", which is slightly different for each one of the sustainability issues. For instance, 60 companies provided an answer related to "Climate Change", while only 52 answered with respect to the topic "Air Quality".

2: The survey questionnaire only presented the nine sustainability issues listed in this table, which often have the exact same names as these issues are presented in the SASB mapping (respondents could also add "other ESG issues"). In order to facilitate answers and to make the results more easily comparable with other similar surveys, the OECD questionnaire merged some sustainability issues in the SASB mapping: "Climate Change" (SASB mapping has three climate-related issues); "Human Capital" (three SASB mapping issues); "Data Security and Customer Privacy" (two SASB mapping issues).

Source: OECD Survey on Sustainability Practices of Public Companies in Brazil.

Specifically with respect to climate change, a majority of large Brazilian companies (those included in IBOVESPA) have publicly disclosed GHG emissions reduction targets, which suggest this sustainability issue is relevant for their business (see figure below). However, only a minority of smaller public companies (those not included in IBOVESPA) have done the same.

Figure 4.9. Disclosure of GHG emissions targets by Brazilian public companies in 2021

Question: Does your company have a publicly disclosed GHG emissions reduction target?

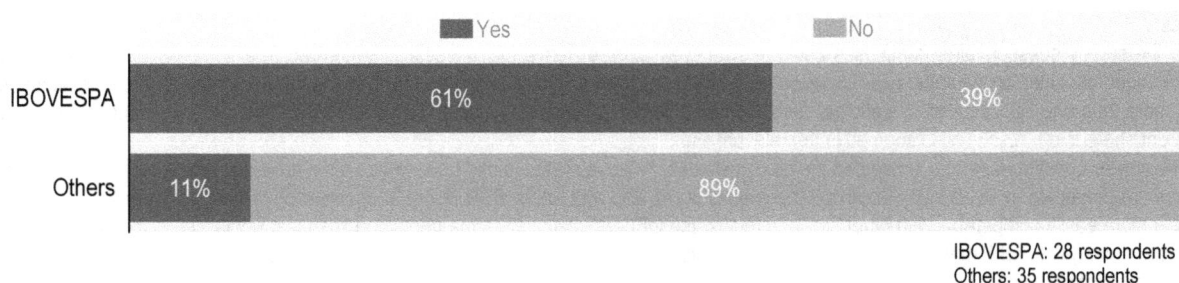

IBOVESPA: 28 respondents
Others: 35 respondents

Source: OECD Survey on Sustainability Practices of Public Companies in Brazil.

An analysis of the market capitalisation of Brazilian companies according to their industries and SASB mapping classification of which ones face individual sustainability risks provides results broadly aligned with asset managers' and companies' preferences above.

As shown in Table 4.4 and Figure 4.10,[5] climate-related risks are financially material to public companies representing 70% of Brazil's market capitalisation (more than the 65% global figure), human capital is material for companies representing 58% of market capitalisation, water and wastewater management-related risks for 48%, and waste and hazardous materials management for 38%.

While ecological impacts (SASB mapping terminology for biodiversity-related risks) are financially material only for companies representing 23% of market capitalisation in Brazil, it is worth noting that this risk is relatively more important in the country than globally (9% worldwide). Perhaps the most surprising information in the table below is the relevance of companies facing "air quality" as a material risk in Brazil (38% of market capitalisation), whereas this has been a low-priority issue in companies and asset managers in the country as shown above.

Table 4.4. Selected indicators for sustainability issues where risks are likely to be financially material

Dimension	Sustainability Issues	Share of market capitalisation of industries where the risk is material (in total global market cap.)		Number of industries where the risk is material (out of a total of 77)
		Global	Brazil	
Environment	Water & Wastewater Management	26%	48%	25
	Energy Management	47%	45%	33
	GHG Emissions	27%	43%	25
	Air Quality	15%	38%	17
	Waste & Hazardous Materials Management	21%	29%	19
	Ecological Impacts	9%	23%	14
Social Capital	Data Security	38%	29%	15
	Access & Affordability	19%	29%	8
	Human Rights & Community Relations	14%	21%	6
	Product Quality & Safety	26%	19%	26
	Selling Practices & Product Labelling	19%	16%	15
	Customer Welfare	12%	11%	14
	Customer Privacy	19%	5%	6
Human Capital	Employee Health & Safety	25%	47%	12
	Employee Engagement, Diversity & Inclusion	38%	14%	27
	Labour Practices	15%	13%	12
Business Model & Innovation	Product Design & Lifecycle Management	53%	48%	37
	Supply Chain Management	24%	21%	19
	Materials Sourcing & Efficiency	27%	21%	19
	Business Model Resilience	7%	20%	7
	Physical Impacts of Climate Change	6%	9%	8
Leadership & Governance	Business Ethics	27%	35%	18
	Systemic Risk Management	17%	34%	8
	Critical Incident Risk Management	10%	22%	14
	Management of the Legal & Regulatory Environment	7%	12%	5
	Competitive Behaviour	8%	5%	11

Note: Sector classification is according to SASB mapping.
Source: OECD Capital Market Series Dataset, Factset, Refinitiv, Bloomberg, SASB mapping and OECD calculations.

Evidently, Table 4.4 cannot be read as the market value at risk, which would depend on an individual assessment of each company's financial exposure to these risks. For instance, a company with a sound strategy to navigate the transition to a low-carbon economy may face low risks despite the fact it is in a high climate-related financial risk industry such as metals and mining. However, in the absence of disclosure of comparable value-at-risk information by a representative sample of companies, the share of market capitalisation in Table 4.4 and in Figure 4.10 can serve as a reference to Brazilian policy makers on how differences in economic sectors' distribution among local listed companies may justify distinct priorities when supervising and regulating their capital markets.

Companies in sectors where climate-related risks are considered to be financially material have a high share of market capitalisation across many different jurisdictions (Figure 4.10) – 65% globally, ranging from 43% in France and 77% in Mexico among countries in the figure below (70% in Brazil). Among the issues shown in the figure below, human capital is also relevant across jurisdictions, ranging from 35% in France to 73% in the United States (58% in Brazil). In the comparison below, a sustainability risk that calls attention in Brazil is water and wastewater management: it is financially material for Brazilian companies representing 48% of market capitalisation, while they only represent 18% of market capitalisation in the United States and 35% in India.

Figure 4.10. The share of market capitalisation by selected risks, 2021

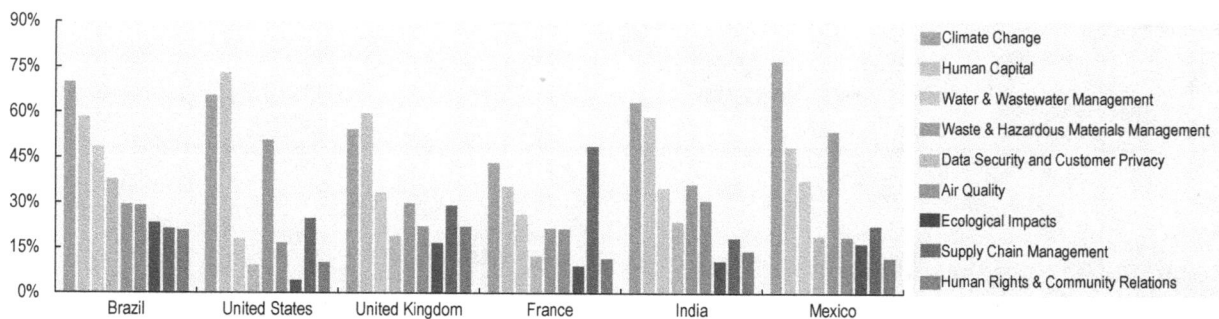

Note: In order to facilitate the comparison of this figure with the OECD surveys presented in this report, this figure merges some sustainability issues in the SASB mapping: "Climate Change" is a merger of "energy management", "GHG emissions" and "physical impacts of climate change" in the SASB mapping; "Human Capital" merges all three sustainability issues within this dimension in the SASB mapping; "Data Security and Customer Privacy" are two different issues in the SASB mapping.
Source: OECD Capital Market Series Dataset, Factset, Refinitiv, Bloomberg, SASB mapping, and OECD calculations.

Existing sustainability disclosure regulation in Brazil

In December 2021, Securities and Exchange Commission of Brazil (CVM) amended its main rule governing listed companies disclosure, including the addition of new requirements to increase transparency on sustainability-related matters. The new rule follows mostly a "comply or explain" approach with emphasis on climate-related requirements, but it also introduces disclosure requirements related to other sustainability issues, such as workforce and board diversity. Disclosure according to the new rule will become mandatory from January 2023 onwards and apply to 2022 annual filings.

In their annual forms, listed companies will need to either comply or explain why they do not adhere to the following practices (item 1.9 of the annual form):

* to annually disclose a sustainability report (if it does so, the company also needs to identify which sustainability reporting standard it uses and in which webpage the report can be found);
* to provide assurance for the sustainability report by an independent third-party (if this is the case, identify the service provider);

- to indicate which sustainability key performance indicators (KPIs) are material for the company;
- to consider in its sustainability report the United Nations Sustainable Development Goals;
- to consider TCFD's recommendations or an equivalent framework focused on climate-related financially material information;
- to disclose its GHG emissions (a company may comply if it discloses its emissions only with respect to one or two scopes, and not necessarily all three).

The following disclosure, however, would be compulsory to all listed companies (with some exceptions for those that do not list their equity in public markets):

- the material effects of the legal and regulatory framework with respect to environmental and social matters (item 1.6.b of the annual form);
- sustainability opportunities in the company's business plan (item 2.10.d) and sustainability risks, including climate-related risks, faced by the company (item 4.1);
- if there are any, sustainability-related KPIs in the remuneration plan of senior executives and directors (item 8.1.c.1);
- the roles of the board of directors and senior executives in assessing, managing and supervising climate-related matters (item 7.1.f);
- composition of the board of directors and senior executive roles according to gender and race (self-declared in both cases), and in conformity with other diversity criteria considered relevant by the company (item 7.1.d);
- if the company has adopted any, diversity goals for the board of directors and senior executive roles (item 7.1.e);
- composition of the workforce – segmented by activity, location and seniority – according to gender and race (self-declared in both cases), as well as age and other diversity criteria considered relevant by the company (item 10.1.a).

References

BCB (2021), *New regulation on social, environmental, and climate-related risk disclosures*, https://www.bcb.gov.br/content/about/legislation_norms_docs/BCB_Disclosure-GRSAC-Report.pdf. [5]

CDSB (2019), *CDSB Framework for reporting environmental & climate change information*, https://www.cdsb.net/what-we-do/reporting-frameworks/environmental-information-natural-capital. [3]

IASB (2018), *Conceptual Framework for Financial Reporting*, https://www.ifrs.org/issued-standards/list-of-standards/conceptual-framework.html. [4]

IFRS Foundation (2021), *IFRS Foundation announces International Sustainability Standards Board, consolidation with CDSB and VRF, and publication of prototype disclosure requirements*, https://www.ifrs.org/news-and-events/news/2021/11/ifrs-foundation-announces-issb-consolidation-with-cdsb-vrf-publication-of-prototypes/ (accessed on 23 December 2021). [14]

IFRS Foundation (2021), *Proposed Targeted Amendments to the IFRS Foundation Constitution to Accommodate an International Sustainability Standards Board to Set IFRS Sustainability Standards*, https://www.ifrs.org/content/dam/ifrs/project/sustainability-reporting/ed-2021-5-proposed-constitution-amendments-to-accommodate-sustainability-board.pdf. [15]

IFRS Foundation (2018), *Who uses IFRS Standards?*, https://www.ifrs.org/use-around-the-world/use-of-ifrs-standards-by-jurisdiction/#analysis-introduction. [13]

IOSCO (2021), *Report on Sustainability-related Issuer Disclosures*, https://www.iosco.org/library/pubdocs/pdf/IOSCOPD678.pdf. [8]

McKinsey & Co. (2019), *More than values: The value-based sustainability reporting that investors want*, https://www.mckinsey.com/~/media/McKinsey/Business%20Functions/Sustainability/Our%20Insights/More%20than%20values%20The%20value%20based%20sustainability%20reporting%20that%20investors%20want/More%20than%20values-VF.pdf. [11]

Morrow Sodali (2021), *Institutional Investor Survey 2021*, https://morrowsodali.com/insights/institutional-investor-survey-2021. [6]

OECD (2022), *Climate Change and Corporate Governance*, Corporate Governance, OECD Publishing, Paris, https://doi.org/10.1787/272d85c3-en. [10]

OECD (2018), *Flexibility and Proportionality in Corporate Governance*, Corporate Governance, OECD Publishing, Paris, https://doi.org/10.1787/9789264307490-en. [12]

SASB (2017), *SASB Conceptual Framework*, https://www.sasb.org/wp-content/uploads/2020/02/SASB_Conceptual-Framework_WATERMARK.pdf. [16]

SASB (2017), *SASB Rules of Procedure*. [17]

TCFD (2020), *Guidance on Scenario Analysis for Non-Financial Companies*, https://assets.bbhub.io/company/sites/60/2020 September 2020-TCFD_Guidance-Scenario-Analysis-Guidance.pdf. [2]

TCFD (2017), *Recommendations of the Task Force on Cl imate related Financial Disclosures*, https://www.fsb-tcfd.org/recommendations/. [1]

Vale (2021), *Integrated Report 2020*, http://www.vale.com/EN/sustainability/integrated-reporting-2020/Pages/default.aspx. [9]

WEF (2020), *Embracing the New Age of Materiality: Harnessing the Pace of Change in ESG*, https://www.weforum.org/whitepapers/embracing-the-new-age-of-materiality-harnessing-the-pace-of-change-in-esg. [7]

Notes

[1] Companies sometimes make reference to the UN Sustainable Development Goals (the 2030 development agenda adopted by all UN members in 2015) and to the UN Global Compact (an engagement initiative with companies on human rights, labour, environment and anti-corruption) in their sustainability and mainstream filings. While relevant, they would not normally be considered as ESG accounting and reporting frameworks or standards per se.

[2] TRWG is composed of representatives from the CDSB, the IASB, the Financial Stability Board's TCFD, the VRF and the World Economic Forum, and it is supported by IOSCO.

[3] © 2021 Value Reporting Foundation. All Rights Reserved. OECD licenses the SASB SICS Taxonomy.

[4] SASB mapping serves as the organising structure for the SASB Standards. Each one of the 77 industries in the mapping has its own unique set of standards, and the accounting metrics in each standard are directly linked to the sustainability themes that were considered to be financially material to an industry in the mapping (SASB, 2017, pp. 16-17[16]). The changes in the SASB mapping and the SASB Standards are, therefore, intertwined in a structured standard-setting process. This process is based on evidence of both financial impact and investor interest, using both research by Value Reporting Foundation staff and consultation with companies and investors (SASB, 2017, pp. 13-16[17]). Any change in SASB standards and its accompanying mapping should be approved by a majority vote of the SASB board, which is composed of five to nine members with diverse backgrounds (e.g. experience and expertise in investing, corporate reporting, standard-setting and sustainability issues) (SASB, 2017, pp. 9-10[17]).

[5] Classification in the table is made from a universe of listed companies consisting of 39 260 companies with a total market capitalisation accounting for almost 96% of all publicly listed companies worldwide. The universe covers all non-financial and financial companies and exclude all types of funds and investment vehicles including Real Estate Investment Trusts (REITs). The primary listing venue is taken into account when identifying the market where the company is listed. Secondary listings are not taken into account. The list of listed companies for each market contains only firms that trade ordinary shares and depositary receipts as their main security. Companies trading over-the-counter and on non-regulated segments are excluded.

5 Sustainability disclosure quality

This chapter focusses on the quality of the sustainability disclosure and main transparency regimes. First, it discusses the assurance of sustainability information and then provides evidence from the OECD survey of Brazilian public companies with respect to their reporting practices on sustainability including whether disclosed information is assured by a third party.

Assurance of sustainability information

The use of multiple sustainability-related and ESG reporting standards and frameworks is not the only barrier to greater consistency and comparability of corporate sustainability disclosure. If disclosed ESG information is not assured by a third-party based on robust methodologies (as financial reports of listed companies must typically be), this could undermine confidence in the disclosed information and the possibility of comparing sustainability reports between companies. In 2019, only 29% of S&P 500 companies that reported on sustainability sought external assurance.[1] Just 5% of those assurances were in relation to the entire sustainability report and, in 40% of those cases, they certified only information on GHG emissions (G&A Institute, 2020[1]).

A global analysis of 1 400 large listed companies in 22 major jurisdictions[2] found that 91% of those companies reported some level of sustainability information, and that 51% of those that disclosed sustainability information in 2019 provided some level of assurance by a third party (or 44% with assurance for companies based outside of the EU). Eighty-three percent of these assurance engagements, however, resulted in only "limited" assurance reports.[3] The remaining small minority offered a higher level of "moderate" or "reasonable" assurances (IFAC and AICPA, 2021[2]).

Eight-nine percent of large Brazilian public companies surveyed by the OECD currently report sustainability information, which is a level close to the practice in large companies in other major jurisdictions as seen above. Among these Brazilian large companies, two-thirds hired a third-party to offer external assurance of the entire sustainability report, which is above the average in other jurisdictions. However, the use of external assurance remains low in smaller listed companies in Brazil (Figure 5.1).

Figure 5.1. Disclosure of a sustainability report by public companies in Brazil

Question: Does your company disclose annually a sustainability report or an integrated report including ESG issues?

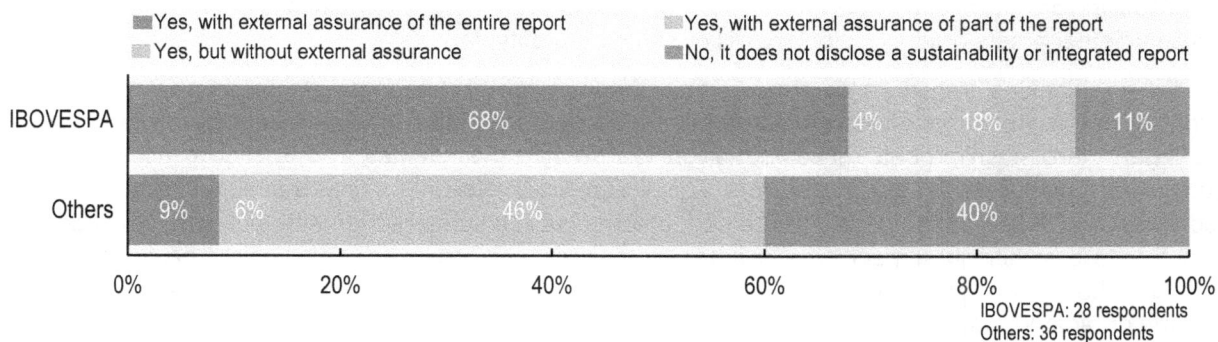

Source: OECD Survey on Sustainability Practices of Public Companies in Brazil.

Mainstream transparency regimes

Financial standards already require disclosure on how climate change and other ESG issues may impact a company's business in some circumstances. A US Financial Accounting Standards Board staff paper states that "an entity may consider the effects of certain material ESG matters, similar to how an entity considers other changes in its business and operating environment that have a material direct or indirect effect on the financial statements and notes thereto" (FASB, 2021, p. 3[3]). For instance, companies will have to consider whether reduced demand for products with high carbon footprints might impact the fair valuation of their assets, and banks may need to reassess expected credit losses for loans to companies in carbon-intensive sectors if a new environmental policy is expected to affect them.

What may be less evident is that companies might need to disclose in the notes to their financial statements more than relevant changes in their balance sheets whenever the information is material for investors, including assumptions with respect to the future. As clarified by an IASB board member, for example, "a company may need to explain its judgement that it was not necessary to factor climate change into the impairment assumptions, or how estimates of expected future cash flows, risk adjustments to discount rates or useful lives have, or have not, been affected by climate change" (Anderson, 2019, p. 9[4]). Echoing this reasoning, an International Auditing and Assurance Standards Board ("IAASB") staff alert highlights that "[i]f information, such as climate change, can affect user decision-making, then this information should be deemed as 'material' and warrant disclosure in the financial statements, regardless of their numerical impact" (IAASB, 2020, p. 3[5]). In Brazil, while not citing explicitly sustainability matters, CVM staff recently noted that auditors should consider, in their assessment of materiality, the "potential of a matter becoming relevant in the future" (CVM Staff, 2022[6]).

As a general rule, financial reporting standards do not require a structured disclosure on strategy, risk management and non-financial information (e.g. GHG emissions) that may be relevant for investors to assess a company's business perspectives and risks. Moreover, management often has limited ability to communicate perspectives for the future in the management commentary to the financial reports and in other regulatory filings. Those features of the current transparency regimes have their justifications, but it is important to consider their drawbacks and observe how they relate to the climate change corporate disclosure debate.

In some circumstances, limiting the ability of managers to communicate their perspectives for the future is a sensible policy. After all, senior executives have strong incentives to convince investors that their recent results were positive and that the future is even brighter: their remuneration and security in their positions depend on that. In relation to past results, there might be some controversy (e.g. if an increase in profits can be attributed to management's efforts) but, overall, books of accounts provide a relatively sound basis for assessing previous results. Nevertheless, the future is even more uncertain. It is often a mere educated guess whether a new product or factory will prove to be profitable.

A backward-looking transparency regime, however, has its weaknesses with respect to reducing the informational asymmetry between management and investors. While the future is evidently uncertain for managers, they have probably invested resources designing strategies and analysing risks, and their conclusions might be valuable for investors. This is especially relevant for risks that do not frequently occur (so-called "tail risks") because they will seldom materialise in financial statements but, when they do, they might have a significant impact on a company's businesses. Those "tail risks" might be financial ones (e.g. a sudden major move in interest rates), risks related to a company's core businesses (e.g. flooding in a major factory), and environmental and social risks.

A number of capital markets regulators have considered the importance of management communicating on material risks faced by public companies, but existing disclosure has been sometimes insufficient for two main reasons: (i) rules demanding disclosure of material risks (e.g. in annual forms and initial public offerings (IPO) prospectuses) do not typically specify which types of risks and how they should be presented to investors; (ii) enforcement of those disclosure rules may have incentivised an opaque disclosure.

Not being prescriptive on which risks to disclose and how to present them to investors has a clear benefit. Different economic sectors face different types of risks and, in some circumstances, even companies in the same economic sector might encounter distinct perils, which may require flexibility to properly assess risks and disclose them. Nevertheless, managers may have the incentive to downplay existing risks because a riskier company has a higher cost of capital and, therefore, smaller market value.

The remedy to the problem above has been to rely on enforcement – by public regulators and through the courts – to discourage directors and key executives from misrepresenting the material risks of the companies they serve. For example, if a company did not include in the prospectus of its IPO the risk of flooding where it has its major factory, shareholders might file a lawsuit demanding compensation if there is indeed a disruption in production due to a major flooding. Shareholders will have to prove that mentioned risk was material for the company at the moment of the initial public offerings (IPO), but what is material in a concrete case may be interpreted in different ways in the absence of a clear framework.

In order to avoid referred litigation risks, senior executives may conclude that it is in their interest to refer to many types of risks (regardless of whether material or not) but, at the same time, use boilerplate language that would not allow investors to effectively assess a company's "tail risks" or competitors to identify a company's strategic weakness. If demanded by regulators or the judiciary, managers would be able to point to a company's public document where the materialised risk was referred to. However, because the material risks were not well detailed, investors would find it difficult to apply adequate discounts to a company's value because of existing "tail risks". Of course, a low quality disclosure of risks may actually mean that investors will apply a meaningful discount in their valuation of a company simply because they do not have access to sufficient information, which would be detrimental to the development of the capital market.

A number of regulators have rules to improve the clarity in listed companies' filings, such as the US SEC in its note to rule §230.421 stating that "vague 'boilerplate' explanations that are imprecise and readily subject to different interpretations" should be avoided in prospectuses. In Brazil, management is allowed to disclose projections and estimates, but they should be (i) included in the company's regulatory filings, (ii) clearly identified as hypothetical, (iii) reasonable and (iv) accompanied by relevant assumptions and the methodology used (art. 21 of CVM Rule 80 of 2022). Moreover, Brazil's securities regulator establishes that all corporate disclosure should be "written in simple, clear, objective and concise language" (art. 16 of CVM Rule 80).

While regulators' efforts are welcomed, there is not any instant and permanent solution to the problem. For instance, an analysis of 2 751 IPOs of operating companies between 1996 and 2015 in the United States found that there was an average 32% – with 41% at the 75th percentile – of text similarity in the "risk factors" section of a prospectus compared to all prospectuses of companies in the same industry in the preceding year (McClane, 2019, pp. 229, 277[7]).

To some extent, the current regulatory movement and investors' demand for better disclosure of climate-related risks might be seen as a way to compensate for a transparency regime that has not been completely successful in informing the market on many future risks including climate-related ones. In that sense, forward-looking information requirements may be important considerations when (and if) a jurisdiction decides to enact a disclosure rule for climate-related information.

References

Anderson, N. (2019), *IFRS® Standards and climate-related disclosures*, https://cdn.ifrs.org/content/dam/ifrs/news/2019/november/in-brief-climate-change-nick-anderson.pdf?la=en. [4]

CVM Staff (2022), *Ofício-Circular nº 1/2022-CVM/SNC/GNA*, https://conteudo.cvm.gov.br/legislacao/index.html?buscado=true&contCategoriasCheck=1&vimDaCategoria=/legislacao/oficios-circulares/snc/. [6]

FASB (2021), *FASB Staff Educational Paper: Intersection of Environmental, Social and Governance M atters with Financial Accounting Standards*, https://www.fasb.org/cs/BlobServer?blobkey=id&blobnocache=true&blobwhere=1175836268408&blobheader=application%2Fpdf&blobheadername2=Content-Length&blobheadername1=Content-Disposition&blobheadervalue2=333644&blobheadervalue1=filename%3DFASB_Staff_ESG_Educa. [3]

G&A Institute (2020), *Trends on the sustainability reporting practices of S&P Index companies*, https://www.ga-institute.com/research-reports/flash-reports/2020-sp-500-flash-report.html. [1]

IAASB (2020), *The Consideration of Climate-Related Risks in an Audit of Financial Statement*, https://www.ifac.org/system/files/publications/files/IAASB-Climate-Audit-Practice-Alert.pdf. [5]

IAASB (2013), *ISAE 3 000 (Revised), Assurance Engagements Other than Audits or Reviews of Historical Financial Information*, https://www.ifac.org/system/files/publications/files/ISAE 3 000 Revised – for IAASB.pdf. [9]

IAASB (2000), *International Framework for Assurance Engagements*, https://www.iaasb.org/projects/assurance-engagements-completed. [8]

IFAC and AICPA (2021), *The State of Play in Sustainability Assurance*,
https://www.ifac.org/knowledge-gateway/contributing-global-economy/discussion/state-play-sustainability-assurance. [2]

McClane, J. (2019), "Boilerplate and the Impact of Disclosure in Securities Dealmaking",
Vanderbilt Law Review, Vol. 72, pp. 191-295,
https://scholarship.law.vanderbilt.edu/vlr/vol72/iss1/7. [7]

Notes

[1] International Auditing and Assurance Standards Board (IAASB) defines "assurance engagement" as "an engagement in which a practitioner expresses a conclusion designed to enhance the degree of confidence of the intended users other than the responsible party about the outcome of the evaluation or measurement of a subject matter against criteria" (2000, pp. 6, 13[8]). It includes both the audit of financial statements and engagements on a wide range of subject matters such as climate-related disclosure.

[2] The 100 largest companies by market capitalisation in China, Germany, India, Japan, the United Kingdom and the United States, and the 50 largest in Argentina, Brazil, Canada, Mexico, France, Italy, Russia, Saudi Arabia, South Africa, Spain, Turkey, Australia, Hong Kong (China), Indonesia, Singapore and Korea.

[3] The IAASB defines a "reasonable assurance engagement" as one in which "the practitioner reduces engagement risk to an acceptable low level in the circumstances of the engagement", while a "limited assurance engagement" is defined as one "limited compared with that necessary in a reasonable assurance engagement but [...] likely to enhance the intended users' confidence about the subject matter information to a degree that is clearly more than inconsequential" (2013, p. 7[9]). "Reasonable" is the level expected from audits of financial reports.

6 The board of directors

This chapter gives an overview of how the purpose of the corporation has been understood and the definition of directors' fiduciary duties in selected jurisdictions. The chapter also provides evidence on the business case for sustainability, in particular related to the link between financial performance and ESG practices. It also discusses different models for director fiduciary duties and investigates their positive aspects and disadvantages. Against this background, the chapter provides evidence from the OECD survey of public companies in Brazil with respect to (1) their practices on executive compensation plans, (2) the flexibility in the interpretation of the directors' fiduciary duties and (3) their practices on board committees.

A corporation's objective

A significant portion of the academic and public debate on corporations during the last 50 years has been largely based on two assumptions: (i) equity investors have the sole goal of maximising their financial returns relative to a risk they are willing to accept; (ii) companies' other stakeholders and society at large should have their well-being properly considered in contracts and statutes (e.g. employment contracts and environmental laws). If these assumptions hold in reality, the maximisation of long-term shareholder value would be the optimal purpose for corporations, namely because of the following:

a. directors and key executives would be clearly accountable to the sole goal of maximising shareholders' wealth within what is legally permissible

b. society's welfare would be maximised when a company increases its profits, assuming that market failures – including asymmetries of information – should have been corrected by the state.

The most famous formulation of the logic summarised in the paragraph above was Milton Friedman's argument that "there is one and only one social responsibility of business – to use its resources and engage in activities designed to increase its profits so long as it stays within the rules of the game, which is to say, engages in open and free competition without deception or fraud" (Friedman, 1970[1]).

Nevertheless, at least since the G20/OECD Principles were first adopted in 1999, consideration of stakeholders' interests has been featured as a relevant consideration, notably in relation to the recommendations contained in Chapter 4 on the role of stakeholders in corporate governance. Moreover, the shift of general discourse in favour of broader consideration of non-financial goals has been accelerating in recent years. In 2019, the Business Roundtable released a statement where 181 CEOs of large US corporations declared they "shared a fundamental commitment to all [their] stakeholders", including to the delivery of value to their customers, to investing in their employees, to dealing fairly with their suppliers, to supporting communities in which they work and to generating long-term value to shareholders (Business Roundtable, 2019[2]). In his 2020 annual letter, the CEO of BlackRock – which is the biggest asset management firm worldwide with over USD 9 trillion of assets under management – wrote to CEOs of its investee companies on corporate risks related to climate change and concluded that "companies must be deliberate and committed to embracing purpose and serving all stakeholders – your shareholders, customers, employees and the communities where you operate" (Fink, 2020[3]).

Evidently, a company's commitment to all its stakeholders is not irreconcilable with its long-term profitability. After all, loyal customers, productive employees and supportive communities are essential for a company's long-term capacity to create wealth for its shareholders. In any case, it should be noted that corporate law does not typically adhere fully to the "shareholder primacy" view, allowing companies to alternatively serve some stakeholders' interests potentially at the expense of short or long-term profitability.

In Australia, section 181 of the Corporations Act provides that directors must exercise their powers "in good faith in the best interest of the corporation" without equating the best interests of the company with those of its shareholders. In Sweden, while Chapter 3 of the Companies Act provides that a company's "purpose is to generate a profit to be distributed among its shareholders", the Act also allows companies to establish other purposes in their articles of association" (Skog, 2015, p. 565[4]). In France, legislation amended in 2019 goes further, establishing that "the corporation must be managed in the interest of the corporation itself, while considering the social and environmental stakes of its activity" (art. 1 833, Civil Code). In the United Kingdom, section 172 of the Companies Act provides that "a director of a company must [...] promote the success of the company for the benefit of its members as a whole, and in doing so have regard (amongst other matters) to [...] the long term, the interests of the company's employees, [...] suppliers, customers, [...], the impact of the company's operations on the community and the environment [...]". In Brazil, art. 154 of the Company Law broadly establishes directors' duties are towards the company, and adds that directors should also satisfy "the requirements of the public good and the social function of the Company" (see more about Brazil's legislation in Chapter 6).

In the US state of Delaware, jurisprudence ranges from an identified director's duty to maximise shareholder profits (especially in some takeover cases, such as *Revlon* v. *MacAndrews & Forbes Holdings, Inc.*) to rulings that suggest that insufficient attention to stakeholders interests may be legally actionable (e.g. *Marchand* v. *Barnhill*). Likewise, in the *Hobby Lobby* case, the US Supreme Court explained that "while it is certainly true that a central objective of for-profit corporations is to make money, modern corporate law does not require for-profit corporations to pursue profit at the expense of everything else, and many do not do so" (Fisch and Davidoff Solomon, 2021[5]).

In any case, from a pragmatic perspective, even if an executive had a strictly defined "shareholder primacy" mandate, the business judgement rule principle[1] adopted in many legal systems and statutes authorising companies to donate money would afford the corporate executive significant discretion to consider different stakeholders' interests (Fisch and Davidoff Solomon, 2021[5]). Except for cases of conflicts of interest, it has been unlikely in practice that an executive would be held liable in court if he or she prioritised within reasonable limits a stakeholder interest at the expense of a company's current profits. The judge would typically defer to the executive's assessment of what would be likely best for the long-term profitability of the corporation.

The business case for sustainability

A central discussion related to corporate sustainability is whether better ESG practices could be proven to enhance financial performance and resilience, for instance due to improved risk management and better strategy.

A large volume of research suggests that the better the level of companies' ESG practices, the higher their financial performance, albeit with some divergence in findings. A 2021 paper published by NYU Stern Center for Sustainable Business and Rockefeller Asset Management reviewed the findings of 245 research papers issued between 2015 and 2020 (Wheelan et al.[6]). This review concludes that 58% of the papers found a positive correlation between ESG practices (such as suggested by high ESG ratings) and operational and financial metrics (such as return on equity, return on assets and stock prices). In 21%, there were mixed results (the same study found positive, neutral or negative results), 13% did not find a clear relationship and only 8% showed a negative relationship.[2]

The aforementioned meta-analysis found a weaker relation between investors' focus on ESG risks and the performance of their portfolios. In reviewed studies looking from an investor's perspective, 33% showed better performance for securities portfolios with a purported focus on ESG risks taking into account their risk-adjusted returns (such as a Sharpe ratio), in 28% the results were mixed, in 26% a clear relationship was not identified and 14% found negative results.

It is important to note that many of the reviewed studies faced methodological challenges such as the low standardisation of ESG data and lack of emphasis of some investment vehicles on financially material issues, which may limit the conclusiveness of their results (Wheelan et al., 2021[6]). Moreover, some other empirical evidence suggests that better financial and investment performance is also correlated with specifically the governance aspect ("the G") in ESG, company fundamentals, and the size and geographical location of the company (S&P Global, 2019[7]; Belsom and Lake, 2021[8]; Ratsimiveh et al., 2020[9]; Boffo and Patalano, 2020[10]).

Figure 6.1. Studies focussing on the relation between ESG and performance

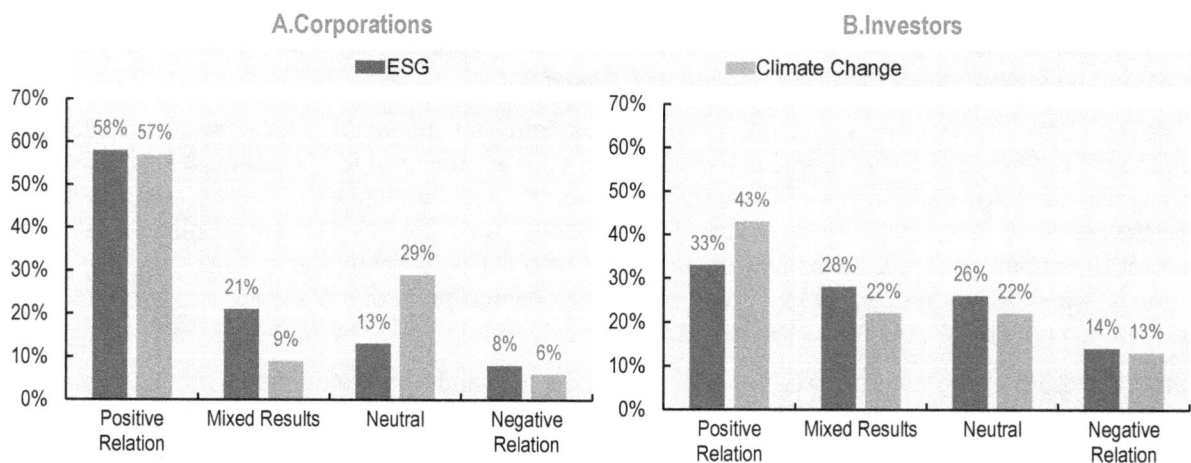

Source: Wheelan at al. (2021[6]), ESG and Financial Performance, www.stern.nyu.edu.

Despite some divergence in research findings about the business case for better ESG practices, companies' attention to and disclosure on sustainability issues have become increasingly visible. This can be seen not only in the high number of companies that report on sustainability (as mentioned in chapter 5), but also in the adoption of ESG metrics in executive compensation plans. While most of the components of the executive remuneration plans are still linked to financial measures, companies have begun to integrate ESG-related metrics in their plans. Globally, out of a total number of 9 000 largest companies with almost USD 104.5 trillion market capitalisation[3] as of the end of 2021, executive compensation plans are linked to performance measures in 90% of those companies (i.e. part of executives' remuneration is variable). Thirty percent of those companies with performance-linked executive remuneration use ESG-linked performance measures in their plans.

Table 6.1. Executive compensation plans with ESG performance measures globally in 2021

ESG scores	Companies with policy executive compensation plans (number of companies)		share of ESG performance measures
	with performance measures	with ESG performance measures	
0-25	1 545	182	12%
25-50	3 224	728	23%
50-75	2 650	1 081	41%
75-100	771	505	65%
Total	8 190	2 496	30%

Note: ESG Score refers to Refinitiv ESG Score retrieved from Refinitiv public companies data. The score is calculated based on the methodology designed by Refinitiv and defined as an overall score based on the publicly reported information in the environmental, social, and corporate governance pillars. For more information on methodology, see here.
Source: Refinitiv, OECD calculations.

In the case of Brazilian listed companies surveyed by the OECD, a significant majority of large companies have their executive remuneration linked to ESG performance metrics and targets (see figure below). There is, however, a relevant difference in the case of smaller companies (those not included in the IBOVESPA index).

Figure 6.2. Executive compensation plans with ESG performance measures in Brazil in 2021

Question: Is your company's executive remuneration partially linked to ESG performance metrics and targets?

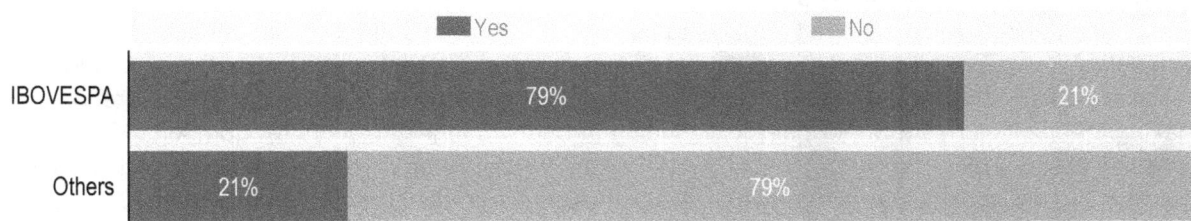

IBOVESPA: 28 respondents
Others: 34 respondents

Source: OECD Survey on Sustainability Practices of Public Companies in Brazil.

Short-termism

A heated public debate has taken place during the last decade on whether public companies' senior executives and shareholders are excessively focused on short-term results in detriment to the investment in long-term projects (so-called "short-termism"). Some have argued that short-termism is not a problem with economy-damaging consequences, which could be shown by the recent success of innovative companies in public equity markets (Bebchuk, 2021[11]) and steadily rising investments in R&D (Roe, 2018[12]). Others, however, disagree with this assessment, and suggest, for instance, that there is a misalignment between executive pay and long-term results that has led to corporations investing less in projects with long-term payoffs such as building new factories (Strine Jr., 2017[13]). Evidence shows that investment as a share of GDP by non-financial companies has been sluggish, growing only slightly since 2005, while R&D has significantly increased during the same period (OECD, 2021, p. 32[14]).

While contributing to the policy debate on short-termism is beyond the scope of this report, it is important to reason how sustainability and short-termism[4] (if indeed an economy-wide concern) may be related.

To begin with from a more pessimistic perspective, better disclosure on climate-related risks and broad legal provisions for management to consider the environment may not achieve much if the incentives for directors, senior executives and investors are to act only on what is relevant for short-term financial results. In the same way financial reports' information on R&D expenditure and capital investment may not be enough to incentivise a long-term view of senior executives and shareholders, it could be argued that data on GHG corporate emissions would not be sufficient to improve corporations' climate-related policies. According to this line of argument, corporations might eventually move towards a lower carbon footprint but most likely only if and when public policy or stakeholders' preferences have a meaningful short-term impact on a company's balance sheet.

In some circumstances, better disclosure of sustainability risks and changes in company law (or at least how the legislation is interpreted) might indeed be effective regardless of executives' and shareholders' time horizons. For instance, transparency could lead environmentally conscious employees or consumers to steer away from an above-average-polluting company, potentially reducing, respectively, its productivity and revenues and, therefore, giving a competitive edge to greener companies. Likewise, better information on corporate climate-related risks might make policy makers act sooner rather than later after realising the concrete physical risks companies face. Lastly, some individual court rulings involving major carbon-emitters may actually have a meaningful impact (e.g. the District Court of the Hague's decision mentioned in Chapter 7).

In addition, such disclosure may impact the investment and voting decisions of investors, who seem to be concerned with sustainability issues when managing their portfolios (see Table 3.1 and Figure 3.4 for global investors' interests and Figure 3.3 for asset managers investing in Brazil). This might be the case either because many shareholders actually have a long-term view, or due to the fact that climate change and other sustainability matters have become a short-term concern for corporations' financial results (or a combination of both factors). What remains to be seen – within the short-termism debate – is whether and how quickly investors' concerns about climate change will translate into changes in directors' and officers' decision-making processes. While it is still an open question, there is evidence that shareholders are making themselves heard rather quickly, including through changes in executive compensation plans. As seen in Table 6.1 and Figure 6.2, over a quarter of the largest listed companies globally and about half of Brazilian public companies already use ESG measures in their plans, and shareholders in some jurisdictions have presented proposals for companies to adopt GHG emissions targets (see Chapter 7).

Directors' fiduciary duties

While business reality is complex, corporate law and capital markets regulation generally present a simplified definition of directors' and officers' duties in order to make them functional. Corporate laws often provide – in a language similar to the one adopted by G20/OECD Principle VI.A – that "board members should act on a fully informed basis, in good faith, with due diligence and care" ("duty of care") and "in the best interest of the company and the shareholders" ("duty of loyalty"). As a whole, these duties of care and loyalty are often referred to as directors' and executives' "fiduciary duties".

As detailed above in this chapter, company laws in different jurisdictions vary in relation to who is effectively the recipient of directors' and executives' fiduciary duty of loyalty. For ease of discussion, one could outline four models (OECD, 2022, pp. 38-39[15]):[5]

a. At one end of the spectrum, company law and judiciary precedents may fully adhere to the "shareholder primacy" view, obliging directors to consider only shareholders' financial interests (e.g. some Delaware's precedents in takeover cases) while complying with the applicable law and ethical standards. This still requires attention to non-shareholders' interests, but only to the extent that those interests may be relevant for the creation of long-term shareholder value.

b. Close to the approach above, loyalty could be largely to shareholders' financial interests but directors would have to *consider* stakeholders' interests, and the social and environmental stakes of a company's activity (e.g. the language in the French Civil Code). *Consideration* here might be interpreted as careful thought given to stakeholders' interests to a degree that is equal or higher than well-established standards (such as those in the OECD Guidelines for Multinational Enterprises [MNE]) but still falling short of what a social planner would prefer for the society as a whole.

c. A third approach would be to amplify the group of recipients of the duty of loyalty. Directors would therefore be equally devoted to shareholders and to a number of defined stakeholders, such as employees and customers. This may imply, in a concrete case, directors making a decision that would meaningfully reduce long-term shareholder value in order to benefit a group of stakeholders.

d. At the other end of the spectrum, directors would need to balance shareholders' financial interests with the best interests of stakeholders (just like in the third approach above), and, in addition, to fulfil a number of specified public interests (e.g. Public Benefit Corporations (PBC) in Delaware and *société à mission* in France).

Brazil's company statute – Law 6 404 from 1976 – arguably adheres to item "b" above. Its Article 2 states that a company may have any business purpose as long as it is "for-profit and not contrary to the law, the public order and the morality". Likewise, Article 154 of the same law broadly establishes directors' duties are towards the company, and adds that directors should also satisfy "the requirements of the public good and the social function of the Company". The same article's paragraph 4 further clarifies that "the board and senior executives may authorise the practice of *reasonable* acts of generosity that benefit employees or the community where the company operates" (emphasis added).[6] In a related provision (art. 116), the company law also establishes that controlling shareholders have "duties and responsibilities with all other shareholders, *a company's employees and the community where it operates*, whose rights and interests the controlling shareholders should respect and fulfil" (emphasis added).[7]

The language in the Brazilian company law, however, may allow some flexibility in the interpretation of the directors' fiduciary duties, and it is reasonable to assume that articles of association permitting a trade-off between long-term shareholder value and societal or environmental benefits may withstand court scrutiny. Nevertheless, only a small minority of public companies in Brazil report such a trade-off would be authorised by their articles of association (see Figure 6.3).

Figure 6.3. Articles of association in Brazilian public companies – possibility of trade-offs

Question: Do your articles of association allow a trade-off between long-term shareholder value and societal or environmental benefits?

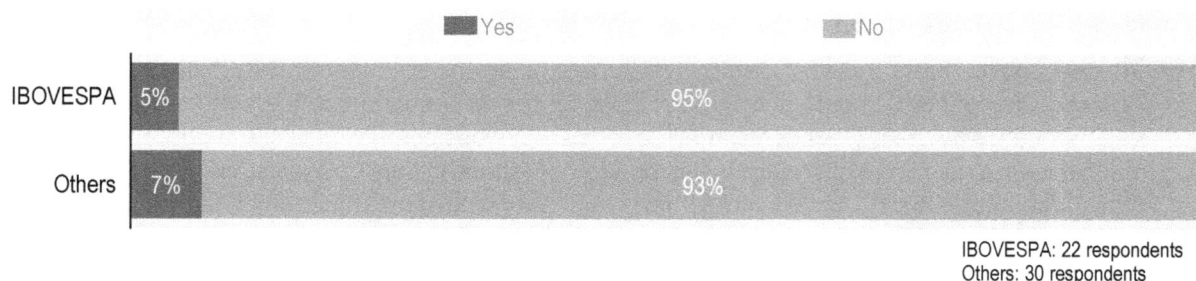

IBOVESPA: 22 respondents
Others: 30 respondents

Source: OECD Survey on Sustainability Practices of Public Companies in Brazil.

Zooming out from any individual legal system, there are positive aspects and drawbacks to all of the aforementioned models.

The model in item "a" above has a significant advantage: directors and key executives are clearly accountable to the sole goal of maximising shareholders' wealth within what is legally and ethically permissible. This model still leaves significant discretion to managers – because what is ethically required and expected to increase long-term value may not be evident – but there are some relatively good proxies to assess management's performance, such as equity prices and profits during a reasonable time period.

The main drawback of model "a" is that, if there are relevant market failures, the maximisation of profits by a company may reduce welfare for society as a whole or even the long-term value of its shareholders' portfolios. With respect to society's welfare, for example, if there are not adequate public policies to reduce GHG emissions, companies may emit more than what would be socially desirable with the goal of maximising profits. In regard to an investor's portfolio, for instance, the wealth created by a profit-maximising major carbon emitter company may be more than off-set by losses in the long-term value of other investee companies affected by climate change (e.g. a hotel chain that would need to write off assets affected by rising sea levels).

Models "b", "c" and "d" – with their own peculiarities – make an attempt at solving the challenge mentioned in the paragraph above. Recognising that contracts between the company and stakeholders are often incomplete, and that the state – especially in developing countries and with respect to highly complex industries – may not always be able to implement optimal or fully enforceable regulation, those three models impose a duty for corporate managers to consider or fulfil stakeholders' and society's interests. If managers have adequate incentives to consider or fulfil these interests, the solution of expanding the duty of loyalty might be advisable because directors and key executives are arguably the most well-informed individuals with respect to their company's risks, opportunities and societal impact.

When compared to model "a", however, the decision-making process of managers and the evaluation of their results may grow exponentially more complex in the other three models because non-financial results are extremely difficult to compare and value, both with other non-financial results as well as with financial results. For example, if a company faces the alternative between upgrading a factory to emit less 1 Mt CO_2 a year or preserve 40 000 hectares of tropical forest, it may not be evident what the best option for society would be. The CO_2 storage capacity of the forest could be estimated, but there would also be benefits – such as protecting biodiversity and water security with the forest preservation option – that are not straightforward to compare to CO_2 storage. Moreover, there would also be the alternative of not adopting any of the two alternatives, which may increase profits and dividends to shareholders. This could allow the shareholders themselves to donate more money to an environmental philanthropic organisation or increase tax revenues that governments may use to support environmental objectives.

The greatest risk of models "b", "c" and "d" is, therefore, threefold. First, managers would need to make decisions on projects that are not necessarily within their expertise. For instance, running efficiently a steelmaking business may have little to do with cost-effectively reforesting. While expertise can be developed internally or outsourced in some cases, at C-level positions and on the board new issues to consider will inevitably mean more time demand from individuals who may already struggle with a great number of responsibilities. Second, while the economics discipline has found creative ways to value public goods and human life, the technical and ethical challenges of doing so are seldom trivial. For example, it may not be difficult for a manager of a European company to assess the trade-off between profits and CO_2 emissions, because the market for carbon permits is active in Europe, but it may be more challenging in other parts of the world. Third, if shareholders and stakeholders cannot properly compare financial and non-financial results, directors and key executives may become less accountable. In the same example, a CEO in a steel-making business may argue that below-average return on equity was due to a stellar environmental performance and not to her incompetency in leading the company.

While the risks summarised in the paragraph above may be to some extent manageable, this could still be costly and present at least one unintended consequence. With respect to costs, for instance, in order to increase managers' accountability, companies may be required by legislators to hire an independent third-party to regularly verify whether management fulfilled their non-financial goals. The unintended consequences are difficult to assess because the number and size of companies with legally actionable non-financial goals – as seen in Chapter 7 – is still small, but one could observe the role courts may have in enforcing a broadened duty of loyalty such as in models "c" and "d".

How common court cases involving managers' duty to fulfil non-financial goals may depend on many factors (e.g. if only shareholders or others have a standing to sue,[8] the standard of review adopted by the courts,[9] and the extent to which a jurisdiction's legal framework is conducive to the use of private enforcement), but the fact is that judges may eventually need to decide whether managers have abided by their broadened duty of loyalty. This control by the courts, however, might face limitations for the same reasons that may have justified – as argued above – broadening the fiduciary duties in the first place. If the executive and the legislative branches of government – with all their multidisciplinary experts and public consultations – were unable to enact optimal regulation to reduce market failures, it is an open question whether professionals with legal-training could do better when assessing corporate executives' decisions. Moreover, as previously mentioned, evaluating trade-offs between non-financial goals may be technically or ethically challenging (e.g. closing a coal-fired power station that is the only source of employment in a poor community in order to fight climate change), and it is not clear-cut whether the courts (or, in the first place, directors and key executives) would have the social legitimacy to be the arbiter in those cases.

Finally, it should be noted that – as well explored in the G20/OECD Principles – directors are responsible for overseeing the company's risk management, which involves "oversight of the accountabilities and responsibilities for managing risks, specifying the types and degree of risk that a company is willing to accept in pursuit of its goals, and how it will manage the risks it creates through its operations and relationships" (annotation to Principle VI.D.1). Evidently, therefore, if sustainability risks are financially material for a company, they would have to be properly managed by senior executives and overseen by the board as an expression of the duty of care (OECD, 2020, pp. 74-75[16]), despite any more complex discussion about the scope of the duty of loyalty. As shown in the figure below, there is evidence that boards of Brazilian public companies (especially in the large ones) have indeed took initiatives to better manage sustainability risks.

Figure 6.4. Board committees responsible for sustainability in Brazil

Question: Does the board of directors of your company have a committee responsible for overseeing the management of sustainability risks and opportunities?

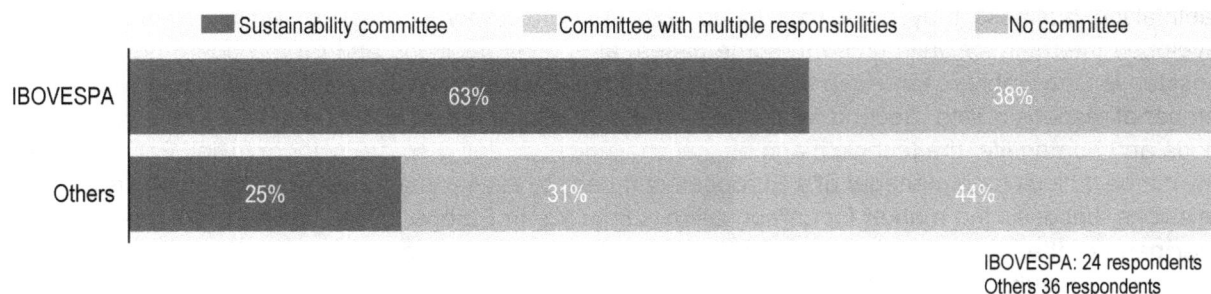

Legend: ■ Sustainability committee ■ Committee with multiple responsibilities ■ No committee

IBOVESPA	63%		38%
Others	25%	31%	44%

IBOVESPA: 24 respondents
Others 36 respondents

Source: OECD Survey on Sustainability Practices of Public Companies in Brazil.

References

Bebchuk, L. (2021), "Don't Let the Short-Termism Bogeyman Scare You", *Harvard Business Review* January – February 2021, https://hbr.org/2021/01/dont-let-the-short-termism-bogeyman-scare-you. [11]

Belsom, T. and L. Lake (2021), *ESG factors and equity returns – a review of recent industry research*, https://www.unpri.org/pri-blog/esg-factors-and-equity-returns-a-review-of-recent-industry-research/7867.article (accessed on September 2021). [8]

Boffo, R. and R. Patalano (2020), *ESG Investing: Practices, Progress and Challenges*, OECD Paris, https://www.oecd.org/finance/ESG-Investing-Practices-Progress-and-Challenges.pdf. [10]

Business Roundtable (2019), *Statement on the Purpose of a Corporation*, https://s3.amazonaws.com/brt.org/BRT-StatementonthePurposeofaCorporationJuly2021.pdf (accessed on 2021). [2]

Fink, L. (2020), *A Fundamental Reshaping of Finance*, https://www.blackrock.com/corporate/investor-relations/2020-larry-fink-ceo-letter. [3]

Fisch, J. and S. Davidoff Solomon (2021), "Should Corporations have a Purpose?", *Texas Law Review, Forthcoming, U of Penn, Inst for Law & Econ Research Paper No. 20-22, European Corporate Governance Institute – Law Working Paper No. 510/2020*, https://papers.ssrn.com/sol3/papers.cfm?abstract_id=3561164. [5]

Friedman, M. (1970), *The Social Responsibility Of Business Is to Increase Its Profits*, https://www.nytimes.com/1970/09/13/archives/a-friedman-doctrine-the-social-responsibility-of-business-is-to.html. [1]

OECD (2022), *Climate Change and Corporate Governance*, OECD Publishing, Paris, https://doi.org/10.1787/272d85c3-en. [15]

OECD (2021), *The Future of Corporate Governance in Capital Markets Following the COVID-19 Crisis*, OECD Publishing, Paris, https://doi.org/10.1787/efb2013c-en. [14]

OECD (2020), *OECD Business and Finance Outlook 2020: Sustainable and Resilient Finance*, OECD Publishing, Paris, https://doi.org/10.1787/eb61fd29-en. [16]

Ratsimiveh, K. et al. (2020), *ESG scores and beyond: Factor control: Isolating specific biases in ESG ratings*, FTSE Russell, https://content.ftserussell.com/sites/default/files/esg_scores_and_beyond_part_1_final_v02.pdf. [9]

Roe, M. (2018), "Stock Market Short-Termism's Impact", *U. Pa. L. Rev.*, https://scholarship.law.upenn.edu/penn_law_review/vol167/iss1/3. [12]

S&P Global (2019), *Exploring the G in ESG: Governance in Greater Detail – Part I*, https://www.spglobal.com/en/research-insights/articles/exploring-the-g-in-esg-governance-in-greater-detail-part-i (accessed on September 2021). [7]

Skog, R. (2015), *The Importance of Profi t in Company Law – a Comment from a Swedish Perspective*, De Gruyter, pp. 563-571. [4]

Strine Jr., L. (2017), "Who bleeds when the wolves bite? A flesh-and-blood perspectuve on hedge fund activism and our strange corporate governance system", *Yale Law Journal*, Vol. 126, p. 1870, https://papers.ssrn.com/sol3/papers.cfm?abstract_id=2921901. [13]

Wheelan, T. et al. (2021), *ESG and Financial Performance*, https://www.stern.nyu.edu/sites/default/files/assets/documents/NYU-RAM_ESG-Paper_2 021%20Rev_0.pdf. [6]

Notes

[1] The business judgement rule acts as a presumption that the board of directors fulfilled its duty of care unless plaintiffs can prove gross negligence or bad faith. Similarly, if a director had a conflict of interest, the court will not typically uphold the presumption.

[2] A review of 59 papers focused on the relationship between climate-related corporate results and corporate financial performance found a similar relationship as identified for ESG results more broadly: 57% arrived at a positive relationship, 9% mixed conclusions, 29% neutral impact and 6% a negative impact (Wheelan et al., 2021, p. 2[6]).

[3] The total market capitalisation of these companies account for almost 83% of all publicly listed companies.

[4] "Short-termism" could be defined as an investment-making process that favours projects with higher short-term cash inflows in detriment to projects with longer-term payoffs, without properly considering the net present value of all possible investment projects.

[5] Some company laws merely mention that directors should act in the best interest of the company, but, evidently, companies are only fictional persons, and, therefore, regulators, courts and other practitioners will have to – in concrete cases – define to whom the company effectively serves.

[6] In the original: Art. 154 – "O administrador deve exercer as atribuições que a lei e o estatuto lhe conferem para lograr os fins e no interesse da companhia, satisfeitas as exigências do bem público e da função social da empresa. [.] § 4° O conselho de administração ou a diretoria podem autorizar a prática de atos gratuitos razoáveis em benefício dos empregados ou da comunidade de que participe a empresa, tendo em vista suas responsabilidades sociais".

[7] In the original: Art. 116, parágrafo único – "O acionista controlador deve usar o poder com o fim de fazer a companhia realizar o seu objeto e cumprir sua função social, e tem deveres e responsabilidades para com os demais acionistas da empresa, os que nela trabalham e para com a comunidade em que atua, cujos direitos e interesses deve lealmente respeitar e atender".

[8] In Brazil, only shareholders may file a civil lawsuit on behalf of the company against corporate officers (i.e. to file a derivative action – Article 159 of Law 6 404 from 1976). However, any shareholder or stakeholder who can prove to have suffered a loss would have a standing to sue directly corporate officers for the violation of their duties.

[9] As previously mentioned, if courts adopt the business judgement rule (as they often do in Brazil), they would review directors' decisions only in the relatively rare circumstances where plaintiffs can prove negligence or bad faith.

7 Shareholders

This chapter presents a discussion on how shareholders may exercise their rights on sustainability-related matters and it reviews how shareholders and stakeholders have been influencing management to incorporate these matters into their decision-making processes. It also provides evidence from the OECD survey of asset managers investing in Brazil on their engagement methods with companies in relation to ESG risks and opportunities, and on their willingness to file an ESG-related shareholder resolution in Brazil.

Shareholders' engagement

With respect to a corporation's objective and its responsiveness to environmental and social trends, shareholders and other stakeholders commonly have three fora where they may influence or compel managers to incorporate climate change risks into their business decision-making processes: in direct dialogue with directors and key executives, in a shareholders' meeting and in courts (OECD, 2022, pp. 26-29[1]).

Direct dialogue between shareholders and management can take many forms. The initial engagement would typically take place in private meetings and correspondence, but it could escalate to public letters, proxy contests, complaints to a securities regulator and lawsuits. An individual shareholder may engage independently with a company's management or a shareholder may choose to co-ordinate efforts with others (e.g. Climate Action 100+ mentioned in Chapter 3 has regionally focused working groups). Despite some differences in their engagement methods, ESG risks and opportunities are currently a great concern to asset managers investing in Brazil (Figure 7.1).

Figure 7.1. ESG risks and opportunities affect your decisions when...

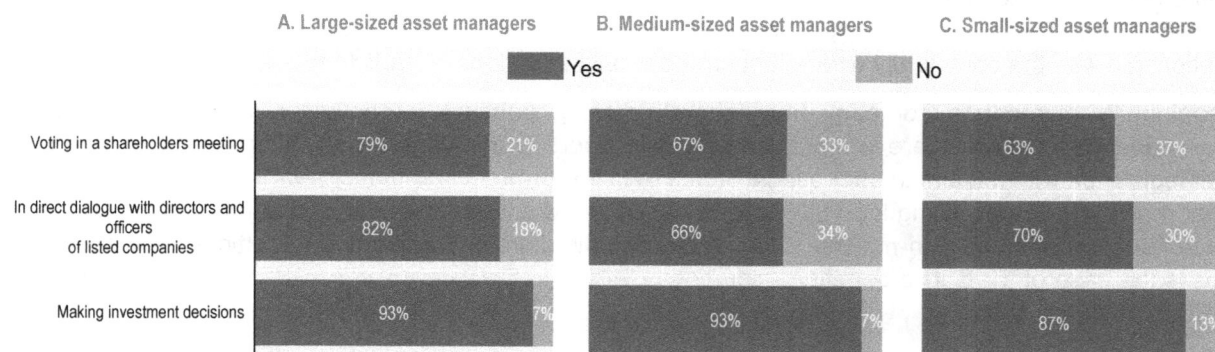

A. Large-sized asset managers   B. Medium-sized asset managers   C. Small-sized asset managers

■ Yes   ■ No

	A. Large-sized		B. Medium-sized		C. Small-sized	
Voting in a shareholders meeting	79%	21%	67%	33%	63%	37%
In direct dialogue with directors and officers of listed companies	82%	18%	66%	34%	70%	30%
Making investment decisions	93%	7%	93%	7%	87%	13%

Note: In the survey questionnaire, asset managers could answer "yes", "no" or leave each interaction type unanswered. The shares in this table consider only the universe of companies that answered either "yes" or "no", which is slightly different for each one of the interaction type. For instance, 60 large-sized asset managers provided an answer related to "Voting in a shareholders meeting", while only 56 of them answered with respect to the topic "Making investment decisions". Overall, on average 97% of the asset managers responded with respected to all of the interaction types.
Source: OECD Survey on Sustainability Practices of Asset Managers Investing in Brazil.

In shareholder meetings, shareholders may typically propose a resolution requiring a change in corporate policy, change the composition of the board or even alter a company's articles of association. As presented in Table 4.2, there were 35 ESG-related shareholder resolutions (five of them involving climate change) among 46 Brazilian public companies in the period from 2019 to 2021. Likewise, a large majority of asset managers investing in Brazil mentioned they would consider filing or co-filing an ESG-related shareholder resolution in the country (see figure below).

Figure 7.2. Asset managers' willingness to file an ESG-related shareholder resolution in Brazil

Question: Would you consider filing or co-filing an ESG-related shareholder resolution in Brazil?

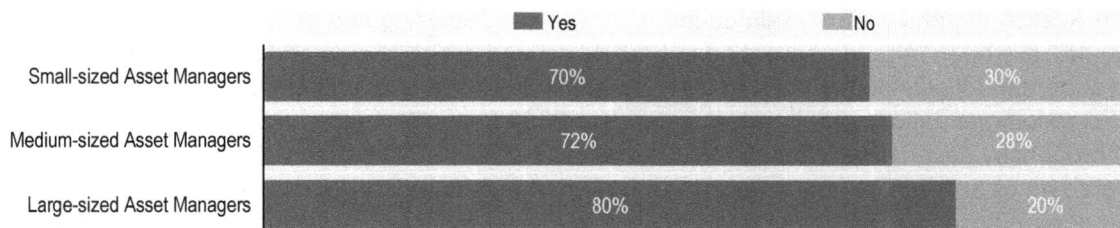

■ Yes   ■ No

	Yes	No
Small-sized Asset Managers	70%	30%
Medium-sized Asset Managers	72%	28%
Large-sized Asset Managers	80%	20%

Note: In the survey questionnaire, asset managers could answer "yes", "no" or leave this question unanswered. The shares in this table consider only the universe of asset managers that answered either "yes" or "no". On average 75% of the asset managers responded within each size category.
Source: OECD Survey on Sustainability Practices of Asset Managers Investing in Brazil.

Shareholders' proposals are often focused on specific issues and they demand relatively short-term action from management such as developing a report or a strategy, however shareholders may also propose amendments to a company's articles of association with broader and longer-term consequences. Applicable company law will evidently affect shareholders' alternatives and needs, but, for instance, articles of association may require a long-term view from management or even explicitly allow executives' consideration of non-shareholder interests irrespective of their effect on shareholders' wealth. For example, Brazilian consumer good Grupo SOMA's articles of association provide the company "shall consider: the short and long-term interests of the company and its shareholders; the economic, social, environmental and legal short and long-term effect of the company's operations on its active employees, suppliers, consumers and other creditors of the company and its subsidiaries, as well as the company's relationship with the community where it operates locally and globally" (article three, single paragraph).

Meaningfully diverting a company from a profit-making goal would, however, create a number of challenges, some of which are further covered in this report. That is why some jurisdictions have amended their legislation with the aim to offer a legal structure fit for for-profit corporations willing to adopt objectives other than simply maximising long-term profits, while allowing shareholders to retain the same degree of control of corporate decision-making, such as electing directors and amending the articles of association. This is the case of the public benefit corporations ("PBC") in Delaware and *sociétés à mission* in France (OECD, 2022, pp. 27-28[1]).

In some cases, stakeholders may decide a lawsuit is the best or only solution to a disagreement with a company's management. It may be either because a company's management was irresponsive to a legitimate request or due to the fact compensation for an irreversible damage is warranted. As a general rule, only shareholders have standing to sue with respect to the violation of directors' fiduciary duties, but stakeholders may have a number of other grounds to bring a suit against a corporation or its managers (some examples below).

Corporations are defendants in 18 climate change-related court cases filed globally between May 2020 and May 2021 (14 in the United States and four in other countries).[1] Climate-related corporate litigation has been traditionally focused on major carbon-emitters (there are still 33 ongoing cases worldwide against the largest fossil fuel companies), and applicants have most commonly argued defendants were liable for past contributions to climate change (for instance, municipalities in the United States requesting damages to pay for climate change adaptation). An increasing number of claims, however, have also covered the current fulfilment of fiduciary duties and due diligence obligations by companies and their managers in industries other than oil and gas, and cement (notably pension funds, banks and asset managers as defendants), including claims of insufficient disclosure of climate-related information, inconsistencies between discourse and action on climate change, and inadequate management of climate risks (Setzer J and Higham C, 2021[2]).

As examples of recent litigation strategies focused on the fulfilment of fiduciary and care duties, a member of an Australian pension fund claimed the fund was not disclosing and managing climate change risks as it would have been required according to broadly defined duties of care and transparency under company and superannuation industry laws. In a settlement in 2020, the fund agreed to report on climate in line with TCFD recommendations and to adopt a net-zero 2050 goal (*McVeigh* v. *REST*). In 2021, answering to a suit brought by seven environmental NGOs and more than 17 000 citizens, the District Court of the Hague ordered an oil and gas company based in the Netherlands to reduce its own emissions and its customers' emissions in accordance with the goals of the Paris Agreement as an obligation derived from the standard of care laid down in the Dutch Civil Code (*Milieudefensie* et al. v. *Royal Dutch Shell*) (LSE, 2020[3]).

In Brazil, an event that has given rise to a number of legal proceedings was the rupture of a Vale's tailings dam in the city of Brumadinho in 2019, which resulted in 270 fatalities and caused extensive property and environmental damage in the region. In addition to some criminal proceedings and public civil actions with claims for damages (settlements so far have an estimated value of USD 7.5 billion), Vale and some of its current and former executives are defendants in a securities class action brought before federal courts in New York that alleges the company made false and misleading statements or omitted to make disclosures concerning the risks of the operations of the Brumadinho dam and the adequacy of the related programs and procedures. Based on similar claims, six arbitrations have been filled before the arbitration chamber of B3 by (i) 385 minority shareholders, (ii) a class association of minority shareholders and (iii) foreign investment funds (alleged estimated losses in these arbitrations vary between USD 360 million and USD 775 million) (Vale, 2022, pp. 21; 173-176[4]). CVM has also initiated an administrative proceeding to assess Vale's key executives fulfilment of their duty of care in events related to the rupture of the dam in Brumadinho, and the indictment has yet to be evaluated by the Commissioners (CVM, 2019[5]).

Shareholder rights

Corporate and securities laws usually provide – in a language similar to the one adopted by G20/OECD Principle II – that shareholders have the right to "obtain relevant and material information on the corporation on a timely and regular basis", "elect and remove members of the board", and "approve or participate in decisions concerning fundamental corporate changes". As seen in Table 4.2 shareholders have been exercising some of those rights on ESG-related issues, such as requesting a company to substantially reduce Scope 3 GHG emissions. Likewise, global investors managing more than USD 10 trillion and a large majority of asset managers investing in Brazil have reported to be willing to engage with companies on sustainability issues (see, respectively, Table 3.2 and Figure 7.1).

What may not be clear in some jurisdictions and in the G20/OECD Principles are the limits for a majority of shareholders to impose non-financial goals and reporting obligations to companies (especially public ones). Arguably the two rights are closely linked: if the central objective of the corporation is to maximise long-term shareholder value, the relevant information to be disclosed would be focused on what is financially material. However, when the corporation has societal or environmental goals together with the purpose of maximising shareholders' wealth, both what is financially material and relevant to those chosen non-financial goals may need to be reported to shareholders.

This section will refer to the discussion on materiality in Chapter 4, and focus on the questions related to the imposition by shareholders of non-financial objectives that would divert a company from the sole purpose of making profits. In any circumstance, the following should be clear: if the fulfilment of a non-shareholder stakeholder's interest is expected to increase a company's long-term value, it is beyond doubt that management should be allowed to fulfil such an interest. The hard question – which is the focus of the following paragraphs – is whether a trade-off between long-term value and stakeholders' interests may be possible.

Something to consider is that some individuals who are – directly or through investment vehicles[2] – shareholders of listed companies are also philanthropists and may have concerns other than their wealth. Even mainstream economic models that assume rational behaviour often recognise that individuals maximise their utility, which may include avoiding an environmental catastrophe, and not strictly their wealth. This begs the question of whether corporations should fulfil their shareholders' willingness to advance the common good instead of distributing dividends that may be eventually donated by the shareholders to philanthropic institutions (OECD, 2022, pp. 39-41[1])

It is difficult to assess the extent to which individuals would accept a trade-off between their wealth and public goods. A proxy may be the value of assets under management by philanthropic foundations, which are sometimes linked to controlling shareholders or founders of public companies, in 24 major jurisdictions in all continents: USD 1.5 trillion in assets as of mid-2010s with an annual average expenditure rate of 10% (Johnson, 2018, pp. 17-20[6]). These assets under management represent only around 1% of the global equity markets, which may signal that individuals' willingness to accept an exchange of their wealth for public goods is low.

Despite its conceivable small practical relevance as suggested in the paragraph above, it may be argued that corporations could provide some public goods (or reduce a public bad) more cost-effectively than philanthropic institutions. For instance, permits for European companies to emit one ton of CO_2 (a proxy of the cost for a company to emit one less ton) reached a record price of USD 71 in August 2021 (Financial Times, 2021[7]) while the cost of capturing CO_2 directly in the air (what an independent institution may do) – without even considering the costs of transporting and storing it – was over USD 134 a tonne in 2019

(Baylin-Stern and Berghout, 2021[8]). In many other contexts, however, corporations may not have any clear advantage in advancing the common good when compared to philanthropic institutions, such as if a fossil fuel company were to develop a reforestation project.

In pondering upon the challenges above, a majority of shareholders have the right in some jurisdictions to eventually decide to change a company's articles of association in order to establish goals other than maximising long-term value. That is exactly what – as detailed above – shareholders may do in Delaware with the PBCs and in France with the *sociétés à mission*. In those cases, however, some consideration may also be due to the rights of shareholders that opposed the transformation in the purpose of the corporation. After all, in many jurisdictions, shareholders have traditionally had at least a *de facto* expectation that the main goal of a company is to maximise long-term value. For instance, jurisdictions could consider the advantages and drawbacks of requiring a supermajority to add non-financial goals, or the right for dissenting shareholders to sell their shares back to the corporation at a fair price.

Finally, companies that voluntarily adopt environmental and social goals will face the challenge of making directors and key executives accountable both for their financial and non-financial performance. As previously mentioned in the "directors' fiduciary duties" subsection in Chapter 6, since the comparison between goals of different natures can be difficult, companies may consider adopting new controls, such as hiring an independent third-party to regularly verify whether management fulfilled its non-financial goals. Governments may even decide to regulate which controls must be adopted in case a company voluntarily assumes non-financial goals in order to protect the interests of retail investors and unsophisticated stakeholders who value the company higher due to its commitment to the environment and society.

References

Baylin-Stern, A. and N. Berghout (2021), *Is carbon capture too expensive?*, https://www.iea.org/commentaries/is-carbon-capture-too-expensive (accessed on 17 September 2021). [8]

CVM (2019), *Informações relativas à Vale S.A. e o rompimento de barragem em Brumadinho*, https://www.gov.br/cvm/pt-br/assuntos/noticias/informacoes-relativas-a-vale-sa-e-o-rompimento-de-barragem-em-brumadinho-e4bd47cf845c4b63928e84ae58627453. [5]

Financial Times (2021), *Carbon price rises above €60 to set new record*, https://www.ft.com/content/c1a78427-f3d5-4b4f-9878-c3e1dffee2ba. [7]

Freshfields (2021), *A Legal Framework for Impact*. [9]

Johnson, P. (2018), *Global Philanthropy Report: perspectives on the global foundation sector*, https://cpl.hks.harvard.edu/files/cpl/files/global_philanthropy_report_final_april_2018.pdf. [6]

LSE, G. (ed.) (2020), , https://climate-laws.org/ (accessed on 20 August 2021). [3]

OECD (2022), *Climate Change and Corporate Governance*, OECD Publishing, Paris, https://doi.org/10.1787/272d85c3-en. [1]

Setzer J and Higham C (2021), *Global trends in climate change litigation: 2021 snapshot*, https://www.lse.ac.uk/granthaminstitute/wp-content/uploads/2021/07/Global-trends-in-climate-change-litigation_2021-snapshot.pdf. [2]

Vale (2022), *Form 20-F 2021*, http://www.vale.com/brasil/EN/investors/information-market/annual-reports/20f/Pages/default.aspx. [4]

Notes

[1] 40 countries are included in the database (among others, Argentina, Australia, Brazil, Canada, most European countries, India, Indonesia, Japan, Mexico, Pakistan, South Africa and the US) and 13 regional or international jurisdictions. However, due to limitations in data collection (for instance, cases filed in US state courts are not covered), referred numbers may not include every climate case filed in all aforementioned jurisdictions.

[2] Another layer in this discussion would be whether institutional investors (e.g. pension and mutual funds) would be able to consider non-financial goals of their final beneficiaries. In many developed jurisdictions, institutional investors are permitted (or may even be required in some cases) to integrate ESG issues into their investment decisions and ownership practices with the goal of maximising financial return (Freshfields, 2021[9]). However, pursuing an investment for non-value-related sustainability reasons would not likely be possible in the absence of a clear mandate from final beneficiaries. For instance, the US Department of Labor holds the view that employee benefit plans' fiduciaries are not permitted to sacrifice investment return or take on additional investment risk as a means of using plan investments to promote collateral social policy goals (Interpretive Bulletin 2015-01).

Annex A. Methodology for data collection and classification

A. Public equity data

The information on initial public offering (IPOs) and secondary public offerings (SPOs or follow-on offerings) presented in Chapter 2 is based on transaction and/or firm-level data gathered from several financial databases, such as Refinitiv (Thomson Reuters Eikon, Thomson Reuters Datastream), FactSet and Bloomberg. Considerable resources have been committed to ensuring the consistency and quality of the dataset. Different data sources are checked against each other and, the information is also controlled against original sources, including regulator, stock exchange and company websites and financial statements.

Country coverage and classification

The dataset includes information about all initial public offerings (IPOs) and secondary public offerings (SPOs or follow-on offerings) by financial and non-financial companies. All public equity listings following an IPO, including the first time listings on an exchange other than the primary exchange, are classified as a SPO. If a company is listed on more than one exchange within 180 days, those transactions are consolidated under one IPO. The country breakdown is carried out based on the stock exchange location of the issuer.

It is possible that a company becomes listed in more than one country when going public. The financial databases record a dual listing as multiple transactions for each country where the company is listed. However, there is also a significant number of cases where dual listings are reported as one transaction only based on the primary market of the listing. For this reason, the country breakdown based on the stock exchange is based on the primary market of the issuer.

The IPO and SPO data are collected on a deal basis via commercial databases in current USD values. Issuance amounts initially collected in USD were adjusted by 2021 US Consumer Price Index (CPI). Initial public offering and secondary offering statistics are presented in this report using the Thomson Reuters Business Classification (TRBC).

Exclusion criteria

With the aim of excluding IPOs and SPOs by trusts, funds and special purpose acquisition companies the following industry categories are excluded:

- Financial companies that conduct trust, fiduciary and custody activities
- Asset management companies such as health and welfare funds, pension funds and their third-party administration, as well as other financial vehicles
- Open-end investment funds
- Other financial vehicles
- Grant-making foundations

- Asset management companies that deal with trusts, estates and agency accounts
- Special Purpose Acquisition Companies (SPACs)
- Closed-end investment funds
- Listings on an over-the-counter (OTC) market
- Security types classified as "units" and "trust"
- Real Estate Investment Trusts (REITs)

B. Ownership Data

The main source of information is the FactSet Ownership database. This dataset covers companies with a market capitalisation of more than USD 50 million and accounts for all positions equal to or larger than 0.1% of the issued shares. Data are collected as of end of 2020 in current USD, thus no currency nor inflation adjustment is needed. The data are complemented and verified using Refinitiv and Bloomberg. Market information for each company is collected from Thomson Reuters Eikon. The dataset includes the records of owners for 25 766 companies listed on 92 markets covering 98% of the world market capitalisation. For each of the countries/regions presented, the information corresponds to all listed companies in those countries/regions with available information.

The information for all the owners reported as of the end of 2020 is collected for each company. Some companies have up to 5 000 records in their list of owners. Each record contains the name of the institution, the percentage of outstanding shares owned, the investor type classification, the origin country of the investor, the ultimate parent name, among other things.

The table below presents the five categories of owners defined and used in this report. Different types of investors are grouped into these five categories of owners. In many cases, when the ultimate owner is identified as a Government, a Province or a City and the direct owner was not identified as such, ownership records are reclassified as public sector. For example, public pension funds that are regulated under public sector law are classified as government, and sovereign wealth funds (SWFs) are also included in that same category.

Table A A.1. Categories of owners defined and used in the report

Investor category	Categories of owners	
	Investor type	
Private corporations and holding companies	Business Association	Operating Division
	Employee Stock Ownership Plan	Private Company
	Holding Company	Public Company
	Joint Venture	Subsidiary
	Non-profit organisation	
Public sector	Government	Regional Governments
	Sovereign Wealth Manager	Public Pension Funds
Strategic individuals and family members	Individual (Strategic Owners)	Family Office
Institutional investors	Bank Investment Division	Mutual Fund Manager
	Broker	Other
	College/University	Pension Fund
	Foundation/Endowment Manager	Pension Fund Manager
	Fund of Funds Manager	Private Banking/Wealth Management
	Fund of Hedge Funds Manager	Private Equity Fund/Alternative Inv.
	Hedge Fund	Real Estate Manager

787

Investor category	Categories of owners	
	Investor type	
	Hedge Fund Manager	Research Firm
	Insurance Company	Stock Borrowing/Lending
	Investment Adviser	Trust/Trustee
	Market Maker	Umbrella Fund
	Mutual Fund-Closed End	Venture Capital/Private Equity
Other free-float including retail investors	Shares in the hands of investors that are not required to disclose their holdings. It includes the direct holdings of retail investors who are not required to disclose their ownership and institutional investors that did not exceed the required thresholds for public disclosure of their holdings.	

C. Corporate bond data

Data shown on corporate bond issuances in Chapter 2 are based on OECD calculations using data obtained from Refinitiv that provides international deal-level data on new issues of corporate bonds, that are underwritten by an investment bank. The database provides a detailed set of information for each corporate bond issue, including the identity, nationality and sector of the issuer; the type, interest rate structure, maturity date and rating category of the bond, the amount of and use of proceeds obtained from the issue.

Convertible bonds, deals that were registered but not consummated, preferred shares, sukuk bonds, bonds with an original maturity less than or equal to one year or an issue size less than USD 1 million are excluded from the dataset. The analyses in the report are limited to bond issues by non-financial companies. The industry classification is carried out based on Thomson Reuters Business Classification (TRBC). The country breakdown is carried out based on the issuer's country of domicile. Yearly issuance amounts initially collected in USD were adjusted by 2021 US Consumer Price Index (CPI).

Given that a significant portion of bonds are issued internationally, it is not possible to assign such issues to a certain country of issue. For this reason, the country breakdown is carried out based on the country of domicile of the issuer.

D. Green bond and other ESG bonds data

Data shown on green bond and other ESG bonds issuances in Chapter 2 are based on OECD calculations using data obtained from Refinitiv that provides international deal-level data on green bond issuances. The database provides a detailed set of information for each green bond issue, including the identity, nationality and sector of the issuer; the type, interest rate structure, maturity date and rating category of the bond, the amount of and use of proceeds obtained from the issue. Yearly issuance amounts initially collected in USD were adjusted by 2021 US Consumer Price Index (CPI). For the Brazilian green bonds, data from Refinitiv is complemented with the information received from B3.

SUSTAINABILITY POLICIES AND PRACTICES FOR CORPORATE GOVERNANCE IN BRAZIL © OECD 2022